WHEN DID YOU EVER BECOME LESS BY DYING?

WHEN DID YOU EVER BECOME LESS BY DYING?

AFTERLIFE:
The Evidence

BY

STAFFORD BETTY

www.whitecrowbooks.com

For information, contact White Crow Books
at 3 Hova Villas, Hove, BN3 3DH United Kingdom,
or e-mail to info@whitecrowbooks.com.

Cover Designed by Butterflyeffect
Interior design by Velin@Perseus-Design.com

Paperback ISBN 978-1-78677-004-2
eBook   ISBN 978-1-78677-005-9

Non Fiction / Body, Mind & Spirit / Death & Dying

www.whitecrowbooks.com

Behold the body, born of dust.
How perfect it has become.
Why do you fear its end?
When did you ever become less by dying?

JALĀL AD-DĪN MUHAMMAD RŪMĪ (13TH CENTURY)

To my grandchildren

Lily
Kaylin
Piper
Adya
Lyla
Beaux

And the little ones soon to follow.
May their interest in the Big
Questions grow with age.

Also by the author:

Fiction:
The Rich Man
Sing Like the Whippoorwill
Sunlit Waters
Thomas
The Imprisoned Splendor
The Severed Breast

Non-fiction:
Vadiraja's Refutation of Sankara's Non-Dualism
The Afterlife Unveiled: What the Dead Are Telling Us About Their World
Heaven and Hell Unveiled: Updates from the World of Spirit

Praise for *When Did You Ever Become Less By Dying?*

Our culture is plagued by the fear of death. How can we transform this fear into inspiration for living and dying well? This insightful work offers valuable insight, reliable information, and a message of hope.

~ MARILYN SCHLITZ, PH.D
AUTHOR, *DEATH MAKES LIFE POSSIBLE*,
(BOOK AND DOCUMENTARY).

Survival after bodily death is a concept that mainstream Western science refuses to take seriously. However, Stafford Betty takes issue with the deniers and crafts eleven chapters of data from various disciplines, each of which contains enough evidence to challenge their assumptions. These chapters range from reincarnation studies to near-death experiences to deathbed visions, to name a few. There is no other book that displays such breadth and depth on this topic, that combines comprehensive coverage with a meticulous presentation of available information. "When Did You Ever Become Less by Dying?" is a question posed by the 13th century poet Rumi. This well-reasoned, reader-friendly book poses a powerful challenge to the deniers, and clearly places the ball in their court.

~ STANLEY KRIPPNER, PH.D.
CO-EDITOR, "VARIETIES OF ANOMALOUS EXPERIENCE:
EXAMINING THE SCIENTIFIC EVIDENCE"

There was a time when belief in life after death was based mainly on faith and unquestioning acceptance of religious teachings, whether based on any kind of verifiable evidence or not. In the present century, the study of the continuation of consciousness following cessation of physical life has become a respectable academic subject, now based on a solid foundation of evidence from cases suggestive of reincarnation, accounts of an apparent afterlife as glimpsed in 'near-death experiences' and verifiable veridical statements from mediums. It is a realm to which we are all going whether we like it or not, and Stafford Betty is the ideal guide to what fact rather than faith indicates that we are likely to find there.'

~ GUY PLAYFAIR.
AUTHOR, *TWIN TELEPATHY*

Quoting Gandhi, Professor Stafford Betty points out that modern or Western insatiableness arises from the lack of a living faith in a future state. He lists 22 compelling reasons why the world would be better off in accepting the evidence which strongly suggests that consciousness survives bodily death and devotes 11 chapters to discussing that evidence. The person who is not bothered – or pretends not to be bothered – by the idea that death results in extinction, obliteration and nothingness will likely reject the book, but those in need of some assurance that consciousness does survive death should benefit from this book. As Betty states, it is not a matter of looking forward to an afterlife and disregarding this life, but in enriching this life by having a conviction that this life is part of a much larger one.

~ MICHAEL TYMN, EDITOR, THE JOURNAL FOR SPIRITUAL AND CONSCIOUSNESS STUDIES. AUTHOR, *THE AFTERLIFE REVEALED*

CONTENTS

FOREWORD

Wᵣhat makes people believe anything? The usual answer would be that they have experienced it with their own five senses. Or perhaps they have been told something by someone they trust, or have read it in an authoritative book. But spiritual beliefs often are not derived from one of these sources. They are emotional passions that have found their way into the depths of our souls. Our inner senses or the reports of others may tell us of events that our materialist western culture suggests are impossible.

As a schoolboy, I was firmly in that materialist camp. The religious instruction lessons were, by common assent, the most boring in the week. We were fed all sorts of fantastic stories from the Bible which any would-be scientist like myself thought ridiculous. Like Stafford, I too read Bertrand Russell's *Why I Am Not a Christian* – but for me it just reaffirmed what I already believed.

But there was a problem. Our family home was close to a gypsy encampment and its occupants visited us regularly to sell their wares. My grandmother, a devoutly religious lady who went to her non-conformist chapel every Sunday, talked to them at length. On every visit, our gypsy friends told her of events from her past, present or future life – events of which they could not possibly have any direct knowledge. How did they do that? Here, for the first time, I was confronted by world events that seemed to defy rational explanation.

I was a sickly child, with chronic asthma and congenital defects in my heart and spine. Our family doctor doubted if I would live past the age of 40. In my 20s, I emigrated to warmer climes in Australia and there met up with a naturopath. I was training in laboratory work in orthodox medicine at the time, so ayurvedic medicine and naturopathy were anathema to me.

But a friend was due to have a kidney removed; the operation was postponed when the surgeon was injured in a car accident, so in desperation she visited the naturopath. When I met my friend again a year later, she still had both kidneys and was in the best of health. So orthodox medicine clearly did not have all the answers. Perhaps, by extension, scientific materialism also had its limitations.

This rather rambling account is by way of explaining why and how I, at nearly 80, having trained in rationalist science and orthodox medicine, have become a passionate supporter of psychic events and firm believer in the afterlife of the soul. I have never had an overtly spiritual experience of any kind, other than as a source of my creative inspiration. I have had half-a-dozen operations under general anaesthesia, including quadruple coronary bypass surgery but never experienced an NDE. I do not "belong" to any religion: my belief in psychic phenomena is purely rational, based on evidence such as the author presents to us here. To suggest that all this evidence is "imaginary" or "fraudulent" is grossly insulting to those who have experienced such phenomena.

For a century and a half now, the experimental evidence has been accumulating that the material world we experience with the five senses is but a limited vision of all that is. There is such a wealth of evidence now that some people can communicate with one another or know of distant events without experiencing them with the five senses we all normally possess. Empathetic and simultaneous experiences of twins are but one set of examples. Some people can even communicate with the realm of discarnate souls in the afterlife. There is nothing morally objectionable about this, though many religious obsessives believe it to be "sinful". Such experiences provide hope and comfort to the living. This book encourages us to create a new paradigm of spirituality if humankind is to flourish or, perhaps, even to survive.

Dr Stafford Betty, in this book, has given us a whole raft of experiences that affirm the continuing existence in the afterlife of the individual soul after mortal death. As well as giving us accounts of spiritual communication by mediums and near-death experiences, there is a more detailed account of poltergeist activity than I have encountered before. For me, this is the most convincing evidence I have read about poltergeists. There is rational discussion of Instrumental Transcommunication, rarely mentioned in other afterlife books.

I have read many books about the afterlife but Stafford's book has a more wide-ranging survey of anecdotal reports with rational interpretations that I find convincing; though possible causes other than spirit activity for these and other psychic phenomena are fully considered. The stories are told in Professor Betty's usual engaging way that has won the admiration of his students in California. There is nothing boring or frightening here. Overall, this presentation gives us a whole-world view, a goal and a purpose to our lives, and an encouraging optimism about what lies before us at its end. Death is not the end of our existence but a new beginning. When the physical body dies, you're not dead, you've just relocated.

Howard A. Jones
B.Sc. (Hons), M.Sc., Ph.D., M.R.S.C.

INTRODUCTION

When Samantha was just shy of her fifth birthday, an age when her delight in every manner of living creature was well underway, she noticed a slug on the sidewalk. This was the same slug she noticed just a few hours earlier, slowly crawling down the front steps of her home. Only now it was smashed on the sidewalk.

"What happened to it?" she asked.

"It looks like it got stepped on, Samantha," said her mom.

"But why isn't it moving?"

Her mom looked at her husband as if handing off the conversation. He said, "Samantha, it's not moving because it died."

She slowed her walk toward the house and looked puzzled. Then she looked up at her dad and said, "Will you die, daddy?"

"Yes, Samantha, I will."

"Will sister die?"

"One day, yes."

"Will mommy die?"

"Yes."

Tears began to fill her eyes. "Will *I* die?"

"Yes, Samantha. One day, a long, long time from now, you will."

Now inside the house, Samantha began to cry uncontrollably. When she calmed down just a bit, her dad continued, "Samantha, I know that makes you afraid. That's okay. But why are you so upset? Are you afraid that if you die you'll miss mommy?"

"No."

"Are you afraid you'll miss your sister?"

"No."

"Are you afraid you'll miss daddy?"

"No."

She looked up at her dad, eyes swimming with tears, and said, "I'll miss *myself.*"

When I first heard this strangely beautiful story from a friend of mine, it almost took my breath away. Here was a little girl who grasped the human situation in all its sadness. She hadn't been introduced to any of the strategies that adults use to drown out the terrifying thought of ceasing to be. She saw the truth raw—what most of us have felt at one time or another.

In this book we'll consider the only answer that would have a chance of consoling Samantha—that, while death will certainly mean missing those she leaves behind, it won't mean missing herself.

Science is king at public universities like the place where I teach. Too often it steps beyond its boundaries and claims, or at least implies, that human beings are entirely material organisms, nothing more than physical stuff. Too often students emerge from their classes thinking that belief in spiritual worlds and beings is for the weak of mind.

But what a forlorn worldview this is, as Samantha precociously saw. Parents and children all annihilated, reduced to nothingness at death. As the celebrated atheist Christopher Hitchens said shortly before his death, "When I speak of annihilation I mean just that the screen goes blank."

Does the screen really go blank?

Hitchens was rightly distressed at the thought of extinction. So was Woody Allen when he wrote, "I don't want to achieve immortality through my work; I want to achieve immortality through not dying."

Like Hitchens, I'm not capable of believing something just because it's written in a scripture or promulgated by a religious leader. I need evidence, and in that way we are very similar. Why, then, do we come to such different conclusions? My impression of him is that he didn't make a serious in-depth study of the evidence that's available to everybody and that you'll be introduced to in this book.

The great English historian Arnold Toynbee was, like Hitchens, a non-believer in survival for almost all his life. But he changed his mind shortly before his death in 1975 and credited research on the near-death experience (NDE) for the shift. The last book he wrote and edited was titled *Life After Death* (1976).

Since his death the field of psychical research has grown far beyond anything he could have imagined. Not only do we get assurance that there is life after death, we even get hints of its nature—a spiritual world more plausible and attractive than any given to us by the world's religions.

This evidence might not be enough to convince dyed-in-the-wool physicalists that they survive death, for they are certain that the brain generates consciousness, so when the brain dies, so do we. My colleagues and I find support for a different view: that the brain works with consciousness as its organ while embodied, but that the brain is not necessary for consciousness to exist when free of the body.

I am confident that Samantha's tears will dry when she grasps the good news her dad didn't get around to telling her. We'll see why in the pages that follow.

A number of my colleagues at the university where I work assume that my interest in the afterlife comes from disappointments in life. They assume it is compensation for happiness missed—an escape from the here and now. They could not be more wrong. Instead, it grows out of a deep involvement with the here and now.

To put it simply, if a society stops believing in an afterlife where its members are held accountable before God (or Higher Power) for what they do, it will tend to drift from the moral and cultural norms that are crucial to its existence. As Ivan said in Dostoevsky's *The Brothers Karamazov*, "If God does not exist, then everything is permitted." This drift, I believe, is occurring right now in our own country, especially among middle-aged men. (Suicide rates for men in their 50's are up almost 50% from 1999 to 2010.) I am deeply concerned about this and want to do what little I can to restore for my readers a sense of meaning and purpose in their lives, especially their suffering.

It's not fashionable to say this, but every society needs moral absolutes. Nazi Germany didn't have any. It was prepared to violate its treaty obligations if they became inconvenient. And they did. It was Himmler who asked the question, "What, after all, compels us to keep our promises?" The answer was, nothing.

The influential post-modern philosopher Richard Rorty couldn't do much better. He, too, lived without absolutes. When asked how he defended his sense of moral outrage at the Nazi Holocaust, he could say only that it was based on his "personal sense of revulsion." But the Nazis didn't share that revulsion. So who is right? Without absolutes there is no answer, everything is relative.

The eleventh-century philosopher Al-Ghazzali, widely regarded as the most influential Muslim since Muhammad himself, classically makes the case against all this relativism. To deny the existence of a surviving soul, to "deny the future life, heaven, hell, resurrection, and judgment" is to invite moral chaos. He predicted that men and women living without moral absolutes would "give way to a bestial indulgence of their appetites."

And that's what's happening—in government, on Wall Street, in our cities, in our neighborhoods. How many sacrifice their own interests when no one is policing them? There are those who say that men and women are capable of policing themselves by using reason. My experience of people who talk this way is that they are often the first to reason their way out of the policies and standards they helped create when they become inconvenient!

We need to feel that there are penalties for our inhumanity. In his book *The Devil's Delusion*, David Berlinski, a secular Jew, makes this point. No fan of the Catholic Church and the atrocities of some of its priests, he nevertheless defends it. "Just *who* has imposed on the suffering human race poison gas, barbed wire, high explosives, experiments in eugenics, the formula for Zyklon B, heavy artillery, pseudo-scientific justifications for mass murder, cluster bombs, attack submarines, napalm, intercontinental ballistic missiles, military space platforms, and nuclear weapons? If memory serves, it was not the Vatican."

Evidence reaching us from the world beyond death has much to tell us about the consequences of immorality. Anyone who has concluded that hatred, cruelty, cowardice, laziness, and chronic selfishness go unnoticed by the universe is in for a surprise.

Millions of us are killing ourselves as we work our way toward the top of the pyramid. Unless we rethink what's truly worth having, we'll make ourselves miserable as we repeatedly fall short of our goals. Ask any aspiring screenwriter desperate for recognition or newly minted Ph.D. in English literature angling for a job in her field. Or, even worse, a "successful" lawyer at a big firm making his half million as he grinds away 70 hours a week and comes home every night dog-tired and depressed. The higher we aim, the more likely we'll be passed over. Too often we feel like Sisyphus rolling his rock up the mountainside one more time.

Arianna Huffington, in her book *Thrive*, would have us find joy in things outside our relentless work schedule. She asks us to "seek a new definition of success that's more sustainable and more humane." "Health is wealth," she says. Which is to say that money and investments are not. Huffington wants to change the way we busy, acquisitive Americans live.

I'm all for the ideal, but it's unworkable if most of us believe deep down that money is wealth, and that we'd almost kill for the things that only money can bring us. The new ideal must be founded on a paradigm shift that assigns greater value to the qualities of the soul.

Huffington sees signs that this shift is underway, but it has a metaphysical side to it that is essential if her vision of a better society is to gain traction.

In 2007 Huston Smith, America's leading historian of religions and a sage by anyone's standards, wrote that "materialism is on the ropes." By materialism he meant the philosophy that denies spirit, soul, the Divine, and afterlife. Brains, yes, but souls, no—that is their motto. Maybe in the Bay Area where he lives, I told myself at the time, but in Queens or Topeka? Everywhere I looked, from the editors of the world's most prominent philosophy and psychiatry journals to my professional friends who styled themselves "progressive," I could see no sign that materialism was on the ropes.

But now I do. All over the place a new spiritual paradigm is emerging. It comes not from religion, but from psychical research (or parapsychology), a purely secular enterprise. In the last five years a new publishing niche has emerged: a plethora of books about the near-death experience, deathbed visions, and especially the afterlife are being read by millions of ordinary Americans. Such works, all growing out of psychical research, and many of them written by professional researchers with PhD's, are proliferating at an amazing rate.

These eruptions of spirit are being studied by parapsychologists who know how to sift out lunacy and fraud. What's left is often impressive and impossible to explain using conventional psychiatric models that deny the reality of spirit.

The new emerging evidence makes the mad scramble for material wealth at the expense of everything else irrational and even ridiculous. This evidence points to four truths:

1. Our planet is not the only world we will know.
2. The sooner we make our peace with death the less melancholy and frightened we will be as we confront it.
3. The key to success and happiness here is not how many things we acquire but the wellbeing we bring to those around us.
4. The life habits we cultivate here, and not the monuments to ego we build, will determine our starting place in the world to come.

Gandhi said, "The modern or Western insatiableness arises from the lack of a living faith in a future state." I could not agree more. When we as a society reach the conclusion that there is such a state, we'll stop feeling the need to crowd every pleasure into a single lifetime. And if we take our spirit friends at their word—they tell us their world is every bit as interesting and rewarding as ours—we won't feel we are missing out on a joy that can be known only here.

That feeling of contentment will unleash the energy and time to pursue the things that matter—family fun, enriching friendships, appreciation of the beauty of nature, reading the great books we never got around to, developing talents we never knew we had, hobbies of all types, and volunteer work as we give back to our communities.

But none of this will happen without the necessary underlying philosophy. I look for the day that our society reaches a tipping point that will stop fueling the drive toward more and more things to clutter our lives with. The breathtaking advances of psychical research over the last decade are helping to create this tipping point.

The next eleven chapters are arranged by the types of evidence that, taken all together, should remove reasonable doubt about the reality of an afterlife. Think of each of these types as a sturdy stick that would require great strength to break. When you combine them together into a bundle, breaking them would require a force hard to imagine. But I am understating the strength of this kind of argument. As you will see, a single well developed case in one or more of these areas is likely to seem unbreakable, and by unbreakable I mean unexplainable by conventional physical standards. Belief in an afterlife where spirit beings come and go will commend itself to all but the most stubborn defenders of materialist orthodoxy.

Teilhard de Chardin said, "We are not human beings having a spiritual experience. We are spiritual beings having a human experience." That means thinking of ourselves as souls having bodies, not bodies having souls. It is my hope that as you read along, testing each stick to see if it will break, you will conclude that death, in the sense of non-existence, is an illusion. As Albus Dumbledore said in *Harry Potter and the Sorcerer's Stone*, "To the well-organized mind, death is but the next great adventure."

We can't know death in any full sense until it comes, but we can get glimpses of it if we work at it. Reading this book is one way to work at it, and for those of you who have given up on religion it might be the best way open to you. So let the adventure begin—not the adventure of dying, not yet that, but the adventure of discovering what "dying" means.

1.

DEATHBED VISIONS

Imagine yourself standing at the bedside of your grandmother who is very near death. Suddenly she begins to talk in a faint voice to someone she sees in the room but you don't see. She tells you that her father, long deceased, is "over there—don't you see him?" You look where she is looking, but of course you can't. "Oh, he's come to take me away," she says while smiling, her emaciated arms reaching out to the phantom. She seems uncommonly alert, almost excited.

These deathbed visions, as they are called, are more common than people think, and they tend to be more frequent when the patient is unsedated rather than sedated. There is even evidence that such visions were the norm before reduction of pain by a morphine drip became commonplace within palliative care.

Nowadays many, if not most, of our loved ones die slowly. They suffer from cancer, emphysema, heart disease, AIDS, or some other gradually debilitating disease and slowly slip away. In their book *Final Gifts*, hospice nurses Maggie Callanan and Patricia Kelley provide a thoughtful introduction to this kind of dying. For me, and I think for the authors, the most striking feature of many such deaths is the visions that the dying have of previously deceased relatives or friends, as in the case above. Those surrounding the bedside who watch such an episode unfold often assume the dying person is "confused." Is she really seeing an otherworldly visitor, or is she just hallucinating? Observers unaware of the research into these visions usually assume the latter. Visions of otherworldly beings, however, provide strong evidence for life after death. And here is why.

With uncanny regularity the dead show up. Why should that be? Why does the living Aunt Adelaide seldom show up? Why is it usually the deceased Aunt Eleanor?

The materialist might answer that it would be illogical to hallucinate someone you thought was still alive. After all, a person can't be living on earth and living on the Other Side at the same time. If you had a vision of someone alive on this side of the veil, that would seem to be proof you were hallucinating and would undercut the benefit you might derive from the hallucination. So the subconscious mind sorts out who's died and who hasn't. It keeps track. And when your time is up, it decks out a nice dead relative, never a living relative, for you to hallucinate, a nice dead relative to take you into heaven when you finally die, and your fear of death then conveniently recedes. Or so the argument goes.

But this argument is not as convincing as first appears. After all, how logical are hallucinations? Hallucinations are made of memory fragments, and those fragments are no more orderly as they come and go in the theater of the mind than the stuff of our daydreams. Zen masters compare the behavior of this mental detritus to a pack of drunken monkeys hurdling through treetops. And Aldous Huxley refers to them as "the bobbing scum of miscellaneous memories" and as "imbecilities—mere casual waste products of psycho-physiological activity." The materialist's line of reasoning is plausible up to a point, but it overlooks the orderly nature of these visions.

But let us grant for the sake of argument that their position does have force. I think I can show, and I try to show my students, that whatever force we grant it for the moment is not good enough in the face of the facts. In *Final Gifts* one of the authors shares the following account:

> A dignified Chinese woman, Su, was getting devoted care from her daughter, Lily. Both were Buddhists and very accepting of the mother's terminal status.
>
> "I've had a good life for ninety-three years," the mother said. "And I've been on this earth long enough!" She dreamed often of her husband, who had died some years before.

"I will join him soon," she said. But one day Su seemed very puzzled. "Why is my sister with my husband?" she asked. "They are both calling me to come." "Is your sister dead?" I asked. "No, she still lives in China," she said. "I have not seen her for many years." When I related this conversation to the daughter, she was astonished and tearful.

"My aunt died two days ago in China," Lily said. "We decided not to tell Mother—her sister had the same kind of cancer."

Was Su's dream vision of her sister two days after her death a coincidence? Su could have dreamed of her anytime, but for some reason did so only *after* her death, though she had been dreaming of her dead husband for years. And if the materialist's explanation is correct, why did Su hallucinate a person she thought was alive in the first place?

Of course, there is always the possibility that Su's unconscious mind could have known telepathically of her sister's death. But if Su had never had any powerful telepathic experiences before, isn't this explanation rather weak? (Most materialists don't even acknowledge the existence of telepathy.) I think the most likely explanation for her sister's appearance is that the newly dead sister actually came (in spirit), along with Su's long dead husband, to greet her and comfort her before her death. That is certainly what Su herself thought. The hospice nurse continues:

When Lily told her mother about her sister's illness and death, Su said with a knowing smile, "Now I understand." Her puzzle solved, she died three weeks later, at peace and with a sense of anticipation.

But there are more powerful examples of this type that involve visions had by dying persons who are awake, not dreaming.

Perhaps the most famous case of this type is reported in Sir William Barrett's classic English study *Deathbed Visions*, published in 1926. The awe-inspiring atmosphere is memorably recounted by his wife, Lady Florence Barrett, a doctor attending a dying patient in labor. Here is Sir William's account:

Lady Barrett received an urgent message from the Resident Medical Officer, Dr. Phillips, to come to a patient, Mrs. B., who was in labor and suffering from serious heart failure. Lady Barrett went at once, and the child was delivered safely, though the mother was dying at the time. After seeing other patients Lady Barrett went back to Mrs.

B.'s ward, and the following conversation occurred which was written down soon afterwards. Lady Barrett says:

When I entered the ward Mrs. B. held out her hands to me and said, 'Thank you, thank you for what you have done for me—for bringing the baby [into life]. Is it a boy or girl?' Then holding my hand tightly, she said, 'Don't leave me, don't go away, will you?' And after a few minutes, while the House Surgeon carried out some restorative measures, she lay looking up towards the open part of the room, which was brightly lighted, and said, 'Oh, don't let it get dark—it's getting so dark ... darker and darker.' Her husband and mother were sent for.

Suddenly she looked eagerly towards one part of the room, a radiant smile illuminating her whole countenance. 'Oh, lovely, lovely,' she said. I asked, 'What is lovely?' 'What I *see*,' she replied in low, intense tones. 'What do you see?' 'Lovely brightness—wonderful beings.' It is difficult to describe the sense of reality conveyed by her intense absorption in the vision.

Then—seeming to focus her attention more intently on one place for a moment—she exclaimed, almost with a kind of joyous cry, 'Why it's Father [deceased]! Oh, he's so glad I'm coming; he is so glad. It would be perfect if only W. [her living husband] could come too.'

Her baby was brought for her to see. She looked at it with interest, and then said, 'Do you think I ought to stay for baby's sake?' Then turning towards the vision again, she said, 'I can't—I can't stay; if you could see what I do, you would know I can't stay.'

... She lived for another hour, and appeared to have retained to the last the double consciousness of the bright forms she saw, and also of those tending her at the bedside ...

The story, remarkable as it is for the intimate detail supplied by Lady Barrett, continues. Recall that the Matron (or head nurse) of the hospital took Lady Barrett's place at Mrs. B.'s bedside. Miriam Castle, the Matron, reported the following:

I was present shortly before the death of Mrs. B., together with her husband and her mother. Her husband was leaning over her and speaking to her, when pushing him aside she said, 'Oh, don't hide it; it's so beautiful.' Then turning away from him towards me, I being on the other side of the bed, Mrs. B. said, 'Oh, why there's Vida,' referring to a sister of whose death three weeks previously she had not been told. Afterwards the mother, who was present at the time, told me, as I have said, that Vida was the name of a dead sister of Mrs. B.'s, of whose illness and death she was quite ignorant, as they had carefully kept this news from Mrs. B. owing to her serious illness.

To complete the picture of Mrs. B.'s passing, we turn to her mother, who was present with the Matron:

The wonderful part of it is the history of my dear daughter Vida, who had been an invalid some years. Her death took place on the 25th day of December 1923, just 2 weeks and 4 days before her younger sister, Doris, died. My daughter Doris, Mrs. B. was very ill at that time, and the Matron at the Mother's Hospital deemed it unwise for Mrs. B. to know of her sister's death. Therefore when visiting her we put off our mourning [clothes] and visited her as usual. All her letters were also kept [from her] by request until her husband had seen who they might be from before letting her see them. This precaution was taken lest outside friends might possibly allude to the recent bereavement in writing to her, unaware of the very dangerous state of her health.

When my dear child was sinking rapidly, at first she said, 'It is all so dark; I cannot see.' A few seconds after, a beautiful radiance lit up her countenance; I know now it was the light of Heaven, and it was most beautiful to behold. My child said, 'Oh, it is lovely and bright; you cannot see as I can.' She fixed her eyes on one particular spot in the ward, saying, 'Oh, God, forgive me for anything I have done wrong.' After that she said, 'I can see Father; he wants me, he is so lonely.' She spoke to her father, saying, 'Oh, he is so near.' On looking at the same place again, she said with rather a puzzled expression, 'He has Vida with him,' turning again to me saying 'Vida is with him.' Then she said, 'You do want me, Dad; I am coming.' Then a very few parting words or sighs were expressed—nothing very definite or clear.

This case is remarkable for several reasons. It captures the awesome solemnity and realness of the visions for Mrs. B. She has no doubt that her Father and Vida are in the ward with her. They have come to comfort her, and perhaps to be comforted themselves. The family has gathered, both the living and the dead. One can imagine the sense of amazement that the witnesses must have felt as they gazed upon a dying woman with one foot in our world and the other in the world to come. The witnesses could not see the ghosts, but the uncanny sense that they were present must have grown on them; one can imagine their goose flesh. But Mrs. B. could see more than her spirit visitors; she glimpsed a light so wonderful and inviting that she pushed her husband aside so she could see it unobstructed. "Lovely brightness—wonderful beings," she says.

Then there is Vida. Mrs. B. is puzzled when she sees her sister alongside her father. What is Vida doing there? she wonders. As in the case of Su above, the death of her sister has been kept from her. If Mrs. B.'s mother has had doubts about the realness of her daughter's visions, the truth has now dawned. The vision of Vida didn't fit with what Mrs. B. knew to be true. But there she was anyway. And we, by now, are probably very inclined to believe she was really there, in spirit.

A word more about heavenly visions. Callanan and Kelley devote a chapter to it—it is one of the "gifts" that the dying give to their hospice nurses and their families. Callanan and Kelley tell us: "Many dying people tell of seeing a place not visible to anyone else. Their descriptions are brief, rarely exceeding a sentence or two, and not very specific, but usually glowing." Mrs. B.'s vision perfectly fits.

Though both types of vision are paranormal, some would say supernatural, they differ from each other. The spirits that are seen are conscious beings. The heavenly place that is seen is where they live, and where we will go presumably when we die.

We will finish this chapter by examining two famous cases, one of each type. The first occurred in 1826, the second in 2011.

One of the most astonishing coincidences in world history were the deaths of John Adams, America's second president, and Thomas Jefferson, its third. They both died, 500 miles apart, on July 4, 1826, exactly fifty years after the signing of the Declaration of Independence.

During the last fourteen years of their lives, the two great founding fathers put aside their resentments and became pen pals. (Their voluminous correspondence would become a treasure trove for historians of early America.) According to bedside witnesses, on the afternoon of July 4 in Quincy, Massachusetts, three or four hours after Jefferson's death at Monticello in Virginia, and an hour or two before his own death, Adams stirred and said in a faint voice, "Thomas Jefferson survives."

Every Adams biographer mentions this mysterious utterance but none seems to understand it. One of them, Charles Francis Adams, Adam's grandson, positively misinterprets it. "But he was mistaken," he says of his grandfather. "The fact was not as he supposed. Thomas Jefferson did not survive."

We know a great deal more today about deathbed visions than was known in 1826.

Adams did not say of Jefferson that he still *lived*—the meaning given to the word by the biographer—but that he *survived*. Survived what? The obvious answer is that he survived death. And how did Adams know? It is very likely that he saw Jefferson's apparition—how else could he have known? Whatever he saw was proof enough for him that his old friend had indeed survived.

It appears that Jefferson came in spirit to pay his old friend a visit three or four hours after he, Jefferson, had died. This type of visitation is common in the literature—there are literally thousands of such cases. Often they are referred to as crisis apparitions, death being the crisis. Adams was not aware that Jefferson was close to death since it took close to a week for mail to travel between Boston and Virginia. But the information he provided was correct. Hallucinations do not contain veridical information.

What a fascinating postscript to one of the most influential friendships in American history—two great founding fathers, and the nation's first two presidents, collaborating across the Great Divide.

The next case involves Steve Jobs, the famous CEO of Apple. According to Jobs' sister Mona Thompson, who gave the eulogy at her brother's memorial service at Stanford, his final words were "OH WOW, OH WOW, OH WOW." From his deathbed he was looking past members of his family into the distance when he spoke these words.

What did he see? Someone not versed in the literature of psychical research would probably not have a clue. But by now we know his words—brief, vague, and filled with amazement—were consistent with those typically awe-inspiring attempts to describe the impossible that some dying people are noted for.

Jobs told his sister shortly before he died that he was "going to a better place." Careful research into visions like his suggests that he was probably not disappointed.

So there you have it—both types. Adams's vision was of a deceased spirit, and Jobs' of the world they gather to.

But neither of these was as impressive or suggestive as Mrs. B.'s. She appears to have seen not only her father and sister but the very world they lived in.

7

Today we know much more about deathbed visions than we did when Mrs. B. passed almost a century ago. We know their main characteristics and their frequency. There is even an abbreviation for them that hospice doctors and nurses use: ELDVs, or end-of-life dreams and visions.

In a recent (2014) study in the *American Journal of Hospice & Palliative Care*, 63 patients near death at a Buffalo, New York, hospice center were interviewed daily to see if they had an ELDV. Fifty-two had at least one during their stay before dying. Some patients described dead loved ones "as messengers guiding them on their journey through death." The article draws a distinction between these experiences and hallucinations:

> The ELDVs appear distinct from hallucinations associated with delirium in terms of the feelings they evoke (i.e., comfort vs. distress) as well as the clarity, detail, and organization in which they are reported... for the most part [they were] a source of great comfort and reassurance to the patient, providing a sense of peace and in some cases a noted change in their behavior and acceptance of death.

The article concludes by saying that these experiences "need to be viewed as a normal transition from life to death."

For anyone interested in further study of deathbed visions, I recommend *At the Hour of Death* (1977, 2012) by Erlendur Haraldsson and Karlis Osis. A more recent collection of cases is Ineke Koedam's *In the Light of Death* (2015).

These dreams and visions are the first of the sticks to go into our bundle.

2.

THE NEAR-DEATH
EXPERIENCE (NDE)

Shortly after graduation from college I forced myself to read a book my Jesuit teachers of theology had not introduced me to. It was Bertrand Russell's *Why I Am Not a Christian*. I did this not because I was in a rebellious mood or found my faith unsatisfactory, but because I was confident it would hold up under any battering and wanted to prove it to myself.

It didn't. Russell sent my faith into a tailspin. To cope, I enrolled myself in a graduate theology program at Fordham University in New York to see if there was any way to salvage the wreck. That helped a little but it didn't go far enough. When I would go home I would take my grandmother to church, prop her up as she took communion, and turn aside when it was my turn. It was not only painful, it was mortifying.

The greatest loss, even greater than the death of God, was the passing away of a belief in an afterlife. With its disappearance my life stopped having any ultimate purpose. I was like the man in Sartre's story "The Wall" who pees in his pants when he contemplates his own death the next morning by firing squad. It wasn't the pain that horrified him, it was the utter nothingness that would follow. That thought horrified me too even though I was only 23. But what could I do? *There was no evidence for anything more.* And I couldn't accept something as being real without evidence. Not anymore.

Eight years later I happened to attend a conference at Berkeley – I believe it was in December 1975. One of the speakers told the crowd about a remarkable new book, Raymond Moody's *Life after Life*. It described an experience that some people had when very near death, so near that their vital signs flattened out. Yet during those precious seconds they were more alive than ever, and upon returning to consciousness they could describe exactly what had happened around them when they were in this clinically dead state. Some of them met a Being of Light that they described with feelings of utmost awe and love. Quite a few called it God.

They came from many different backgrounds yet had remarkably similar experiences: separation from their body, traveling at rapid speed through something like a dark tunnel, meeting deceased relatives and friends, a life review, beautiful landscapes, and, for the lucky few, immersion in that glorious Being of Light.

They all, even those who had been atheists, said they were not their physical body, and death was not the end. The skeptic in me of course wanted evidence they were not all hallucinating. And they provided it. Many of them described what they saw while out of their bodies, some in places distant from where their body lay. And what they claimed they saw was corroborated by witnesses.

Many books on the NDE have appeared since then, and they all report the same kind of data as in Moody's landmark study. But what does all this evidence tell us about an afterlife?

To begin with, if you can get out of your body and still move about and see and be aware of yourself as the person you are, then you're not your body. And if you're not your body, then the body's death doesn't mean *you* have to die. And if you don't, but are never seen again on earth, you must go somewhere else and live there. That experience would be what we call an afterlife.

On the surface, the many books and several organizations devoted to afterlife study and research make a powerful case for survival of bodily death, and the best of this literature seems even to tell us a little about the nature of the afterlife that we survive into.

Before developing an argument for survival based on NDE research, we'll need to look at a few cases. I've selected four:

The first, reported by the famous Swiss psychiatrist Carl Jung, predates Moody's book. The phrase "near-death experience," invented by

Moody, was unknown in 1952, the latest that the case could have occurred. For us this is a blessing: No one can claim today that this particular NDE, which Jung referred to as "an extremely strange thing," was manufactured by an expectation broadly available in the culture—what might be called a copycat NDE.

The experiencer was a young woman who nearly died following a forceps delivery. After her recovery she told Jung what she had experienced, and he asked her to record her experience.

Jung introduces the case in these words: "I would like to give an example from my own medical experience. A woman patient, whose reliability and truthfulness I have no reason to doubt, told me that her first birth was very difficult." The NDE begins in a manner that all current NDE researchers are familiar with:

> The next thing she was aware of was that, without feeling her body and its position, she was *looking down* from a point in the ceiling and could see everything going on in the room below her: she saw herself lying in the bed, deadly pale, with closed eyes. Beside her stood the nurse.

As she looked down, she watched a flustered doctor pacing the floor and her mother and her husband looking on with alarm. Simultaneously she was aware of "a glorious, park-like landscape shining in the brightest colors and, in particular, an emerald green meadow with short grass which sloped gently upwards beyond a wrought-iron gate leading into the park." She was certain this scene of "indescribable splendor" was the world she would enter at death but also that she would not die. She was so certain of her recovery that "she found the agitation of the doctor and the distress of her relatives stupid and out of place." All together she was unconscious for about thirty minutes.

On coming to, she "described in full detail what had happened during the coma" and forced the nurse to admit the doctor had been "hysterical." The patient "had perceived the events exactly as they happened in reality.

Jung was most impressed by the coincidence between what the comatose patient observed and what actually happened in the room. He was certain the woman "was in a coma and ought to have had a complete psychic black-out and had been altogether incapable of clear observation and sound judgment," yet she saw everything that happened. Not only that, "she saw the whole situation from above, as though 'her eyes were in the ceiling,' as she put it."

This case is typical of many NDEs. The woman is in a deep coma yet can see what is going on around her, and later reports it accurately. She not only reports it, but reports it from a vantage point above her body. She is not in her body, but out of it. Features of a more developed NDE are missing, such as meeting deceased relatives, undergoing a life review, and seeing a being of light. But what she does see is quite special and of great interest to us. She seems to have gotten a glimpse of a world that resembles ours but is far more glorious—what we might call an "afterworld" where the afterlife is lived.

The next case, which took place in 1958, was recorded by Professor Kenneth Ring. It is one of the best descriptions of the Being of Light in the literature. The experiencer "had an allergic reaction to a drug while giving birth." Here is her account:

> By my side there was a Being with a magnificent presence. I could not see an exact form, but instead, a radiation of light that lit up everything about me and spoke with a voice that held the deepest tenderness one can ever imagine. . . .
>
> It seemed whole Truths revealed themselves to me. Waves of thought, ideas greater and purer than I had ever tried to figure out, came to me. Thoughts, clear without effort revealed themselves in total wholeness, although not in logical sequence. I, of course, being in that magnificent Presence, understood it all. . . .
>
> As this occurred, an intensity of feeling rushed through me, as if the light that surrounded that Being was bathing me, penetrating every part of me. As I absorbed the energy, I sensed what I can only describe as bliss. That is such a little word, but the feeling was dynamic, rolling, magnificent, ecstatic—*Bliss*. It whirled around me and, entering my chest, flowed thought me, and I was immersed in love and awareness for ineffable time.

Many NDEs highlight the Being of Light. The Being usually has no shape that would identify it as a person, yet the feelings aroused in the experiencer are intensely personal and point away from it being a kind of Force. Forces don't love and understand. Whatever the nature of the Being (many experiencers name it God), it is clear they are contacting a highly evolved being with personal qualities. Or at least that is the way the Being feels to them.

The next experience is of great interest to us for its impact on the experiencer's later life. Dr. Rajiv Parti, a successful and wealthy cardio-anesthesiologist who came to America from India to practice medicine, describes himself as an insensitive, uncompassionate man who put his own needs over his family and his patients. He had all the accoutrements of a wealthy Hindu Indian who had "made it" in America: the 10,000 square foot mansion, the Mercedes and Hummer in the driveway, and a reputation as one of the world's best in his field. Along with that came a pretty wife from good family and two sons whom he, by his own admission, would sometimes emotionally abuse.

Here is his account, told in third person and available on his web site:

Dr. Parti's near death experience took place Christmas Day 2010, two years after surgery that successfully eliminated cancer from his body. A follow up surgery led to an abdominal infection that required several more surgeries, leading Dr. Parti to become addicted to pain pills and anti-depressants. Still the infection got worse. Rushed 100 miles to UCLA hospital with a 105-degree temperature and an infection that had spread to his blood, Dr. Parti feared this may be his last night on earth.

Dr. Parti checked in to UCLA hospital where his doctor tried to fight the blood infection with powerful antibiotics. Deeply concerned by the infection's lack of response, surgery was ordered for the next day, a Christmas present that amounted to a lengthy abdominal operation and a near-death experience that changed his life.

Twenty minutes after surgery started, Dr. Parti found himself floating near the ceiling of the operating theatre. With all of his senses intact, Dr. Parti watched as the surgeons cleaned infection from his abdomen. He even heard the anesthesiologist tell a dirty joke that he repeated back to him later. Dr. Parti's consciousness had left his body.

Humor turned to horror as Dr. Parti went to a pitch-dark realm, infused with the smell of burning meat and raucous with the sounds of crying souls. Hell! Dr. Parti had gone to Hell for neglecting the emotional needs of his patients and family. On the brink of Hell, Dr. Parti cried for help, and an unlikely soul appeared –his father.

Dr. Parti's father appeared, looking younger than when he died 20 years earlier –and wiser.

His father led Dr. Parti away from Hell and through a tunnel and then he disappeared. Alone on the other side Dr. Parti witnessed two past lives, each of which provided understanding into problems he had now, his addiction and his sense of entitlement. With these revelations behind him, Dr. Parti wanted an opportunity to change his ways.

He moved through another tunnel and was greeted by his guardian angels who imparted divine knowledge. After promising they would always be with him, the angels directed Dr. Parti to a Light Being brighter than a thousand suns. Before the Light Being, Dr. Parti was given a new direction in life, to help people battle the diseases of the soul – the same ones he had himself!

When Dr. Parti's consciousness returned to his body, his mental, behavioral and psychological priorities changed dramatically. In the weeks that followed, Dr. Parti abandoned his career, and with the support of his wife and children, downsized his family home from a 10,000 square foot mansion to a modest home. He traded in his Hummer and Mercedes for a Toyota hybrid and now spends his time volunteering for community projects and teaching that chronic pain, addiction, and depression are "diseases of the soul." In a radical departure from his conventional medical training, Dr. Parti now advocates a consciousness-based approach to healing.

It is hard to imagine a man more transformed that Rajiv Parti. Following his NDE he gave up his lucrative career as an anesthesiologist, became an advocate for Ayurvedic medicine, started to meditate, and became a caring father and husband. To his wife's astonishment, he even started to write poetry. "Forgive, love, and heal" became his mantra—especially forgive. Today what he wants most is the opportunity to serve. Seva is the Sanskrit word for service, or more accurately, selfless service. That is what he lives for.

What his example means for us as we look for evidence of an afterlife will become clear as we conclude this chapter.

The last example is, for me, the most remarkable. From an evidential standpoint, there is no other in the literature to match it. Vicki Umipeg's story is recounted by Kenneth Ring and Sharon Cooper in their unique study of NDEs in blind people titled *Mindsight*, published in 1999.

Vicki was born blind. When asked if she could see anything, she replied, "Nothing, never. No light, no shadows, no nothing, ever. . . . I've never been able to understand even the concept of light." But she would see more than light when, at the age of 12 following an appendectomy, and again at 22 following a car crash, she had an NDE.

Her second NDE is unusually well developed; it contains almost all the features of an ideal case. She rises out of her body and goes to a place "surrounded by trees and flowers and a vast number of people. . . . Everybody there was made of light. And I was made of light. What the light conveyed was love. There was love everywhere." She meets four of her deceased friends and her deceased grandmother "who essentially raised her" but also abused her. She is flooded with a sense of "total knowledge," of understanding everything, even "about calculus, and about the way planets were made." She sees, standing near her, a figure of light whose radiance is far greater than any of the others and she takes him to be Jesus. This being greets her lovingly but tells her she can't stay, to her great disappointment. The NDE closes with "a complete panoramic review of her life" in which she is helped to "understand the significance of her actions and their repercussions."

But none of this compares to the central fact of the case: While in her body, she can see nothing, but once outside her body, she can see everything that anyone else can see. Of particular interest is her surprising account of what it was like to see for the first time during her first NDE:

> Vicki: I was shocked. I was totally in awe. I mean, I can't even describe it because I thought, "So that's what it's like!" . . . It was very discomforting to tell you the truth. It was not a pleasant thing at first. It was rather scary. I couldn't relate to it.

> Interviewer: It sounds like it was disturbing to you.

> Vicki: It was frightening.

> Interviewer: Frightening? More than a distraction, then? Frightening?

> Vicki: Yeah, because it was like I couldn't understand what was happening. . . . It was scary at first. Then I liked it and it was OK.

Just as interesting is her description of color during her second NDE:

> It was different brightnesses. That's all I know how to describe it as. And different shades. . . . But I don't know. Because I don't know how to

relate to color, but I know it was different shades of light. . . . [Flowers] were different brightnesses of light.

There is much more of interest about her second NDE, but we have seen enough to build a case for an afterlife based on these four accounts, bearing in mind that there are thousands more in NDE literature, much of it available online.

First let's summarize: In a typical well-developed NDE, a person is jerked out of this life into another locale, then jerked back into this life from that locale. In between the jerks, the NDE unfolds. We are now familiar with its main features: the sense of being out of one's body, traveling down a tunnel, meeting deceased relatives or other spirits, undergoing a life review, meeting and possibly merging with an intimately knowing and loving Being of Light, glimpsing an afterworld of extraordinary beauty, and so forth.

NDErs who merge with this Light often tell us the main purpose of life is to grow in love, while a secondary one is to grow in knowledge and wisdom. They come out of their experience deeply changed, eager to accept the challenge of living on, exhilarated by the second chance they've been given. And they are completely sure that death is not the end but that they live on into another world. More than a few have written books in the hope of convincing the world of this truth. A few, like Dr. Eben Alexander, the celebrated neurosurgeon whose NDE changed him from a scientifically trained skeptic to a prophet of this higher truth, travel from conference to conference trying to persuade all who will listen.

What are we to make of their claims? First, if the NDE is a real experience and not some sort of hallucination, life after death is strongly indicated. If you can get out of your body and still move about and see and be aware of yourself as the person you are, then you're not your body. And if you're not your body, then the body's death doesn't mean *you* have to die. This line of reasoning seems obvious enough.

But what if the NDE, including the out-of-body experience, is a hallucination? In that case the experience isn't any more real than a dream, and the NDE completely fails as evidence of an afterlife. So the question comes down to this: What are the reasons for thinking the NDE is an experience of real things, and what are the countervailing reasons for thinking it's just a vivid dream, a hallucination spun off by a confused or disoriented brain? In which direction does an open minded, evenhanded analysis take us?

In a 2001 article in *The Lancet*, the British equivalent of *The Journal of the American Medical Association*, the Dutch physician and NDE researcher Pim van Lommel presented evidence inconsistent with traditional materialist explanations that anchor the NDE in brain states. He explains:

> When the heart stops beating, blood flow stops within a second. Then, 6.5 seconds later, EEG [brain] activity starts to change due to the shortage of oxygen. After 15 seconds there is a straight, flat line and the electrical activity in the cerebral cortex has disappeared completely.

It is during this shutdown of the brain that NDEs, with all their vivid imagery, occur, and according to the physicalist worldview there is no explaining how this could happen. Such "hallucinations" should be impossible.

But if the NDE is *not* produced by the brain, then a non-functioning brain should be no barrier to the experience. The evidence turned up by NDE pioneers like Van Lommel suggests with great force that the brain is not the producer of the NDE, or any other conscious state for that matter, but is the self's instrument and transmitter. He compares the brain "to a television set that tunes into specific electromagnetic waves and converts them into image and sound." If the TV is damaged, it won't work correctly, but the waves are still present. It's the same with consciousness, he says. Our consciousness is undamaged but cannot express itself in the normal way because its transmitter, the brain, is damaged. Put another way, it's as if our computer gets a virus and our messages are all jumbled up. The problem is not in ourselves but in the computer.

Let's look back at our four NDEs: In the first case, Jung's patient had a sharply defined out-of-body experience as she watched from the ceiling while the medical staff tried to save her. She sees a glorious world as the NDE develops, yet throughout the experience she is in a deep coma; Jung thought there was every reason to conclude that her brain was shut down. If so, then her brain was not producing the experience. Something else was.

In the second case, Professor Ring's subject was enjoying the most profound, life-altering experience of her life at the very time that her brain had ceased to function. All of us look at persons with damaged or sick brains, as in Alzheimer's, and conclude that the brain is the cause of the person "not being herself." It's logical, then, to assume that a brain that's so sick or damaged that it doesn't function at all would produce no person at all. But, to our surprise, exactly the opposite happens during an NDE, and in some cases, like this woman's, the greatest of all experiences coincides with the brain's complete shutdown. The NDE is a fact, and something other than the brain must be the cause of it. Materialists are not willing to live with this surprise. I am, and for me and others like me, there is nothing surprising about this anymore, for it has become clear what is happening.

Some people live with reckless abandon; it's almost as if they think death doesn't apply to them, as if there were no such thing as death. Materialists live as if there is no such thing as life *following* death. Given the evidence, both positions are irrational.

In the third case, Dr. Parti's life following his NDE was completely changed. The power of his NDE, the sheer reality of it, led him to abandon his lucrative career, sell his house, reorient himself to a life of service, and write books to spread abroad the saving news. Here is what the materialist needs to consider: Do hallucinations have the power to bring about such radical change? Those of you who have experienced one know they don't.

Many years ago, at a time when most Americans knew little or nothing of the NDE, one of my colleagues had a relatively undeveloped NDE during a heart attack. It amounted to little more than an out-of-body experience. At the time he was, as he put it, a wishy-washy Methodist who never gave a thought to what might follow death. Nothing in his religious training had prepared him for his NDE. It took him two years to come to terms with it and, when he did, he wrote a brilliant and lengthy account of it which he shared with me in confidence. After I read it I got the courage to ask him if he believed in an afterlife. "No, I don't believe," he said, "I *know*." He knew because his experience *felt real*. This claim is typical. A Catholic priest who had an NDE following a severe heart attack told his interviewer,

> Listen, I don't want to be flippant with you, but if I tell you that I went through that door to that corridor [while out of my body], don't tell me that my endorphins exploded or there was a re-uptake or something, because I went through that door. This happened. It was not a dream. It was not an illusion or a fantasy. This happened.

One after another, NDErs insist that their experience was real and that life does not end at what we call death. Over and over they say they no longer fear death. Again I ask, does a hallucination have the power to bring about such a fundamental reordering of outlook? Many NDErs look at their materialist friends and remember that they were "once like that." And they are confident that if their friends had an NDE, they would change their minds too.

I have always been impressed by the NDEr's deep certainty of an afterlife. They, and not the materialists who scoff, are the experts. We are wise to listen to them.

In the fourth case we come up against a case that comes close to sealing the deal. Vicki is blind from birth yet sees for the first time during her NDE at the age of twelve. Consider what materialists are up against. Their only explanation for the NDE—for all NDEs—is the hallucination hypothesis: The NDEr is simply projecting visual fragments drawn from memories in her brain that somehow leak out and create a weird world that is experienced as real. But in the case of Vicki, and other blind NDErs, there are no visual fragments to remember: Vicki sees things that her brain cannot produce. So what does the *seeing* in Vicki? Whatever it is, it's not the brain. This is powerful evidence that she, and we, are not our bodies, and that therefore our brains are not the producers of our conscious state. True, they *are* involved in the processes of knowing and feeling when our brains are functioning normally, as we all know. But apparently they function as the instruments of something more basic—our real selves, our knowing consciousness, our souls, which, under extreme circumstances, can take leave of the brain and see and hear without its help and, more than that, can see and hear because there is a momentary freedom from the brain's influence. It follows from a close examination of the NDE that we are at our best, not when our brain is functioning at full speed and under ideal conditions, but when it *butts out altogether*. Amazing! But apparently true.

The main conclusions we can draw from the NDE is that we are not our body and that therefore there is nothing that requires us to die when our body dies. All indications are that NDErs would have continued to carry on as themselves in a world of spirit if they had died. Not only that, but some experiencers are quite sure they have gotten a glimpse of that world, including some of its inhabitants. Can we trust them? Why shouldn't we? They have given us veridical information about *our* world when out of their body—in other words, they were not hallucinating our world—so why should they start hallucinating while out of their body in this new world? It is logical to conclude that if these mysterious new sense organs (whatever they might consist of) can see real things in our world, they should also be able to see real things in the world they visit. We can't be sure of this, but this is a reasonable conclusion and, if we are correct in our conclusion, then the world of light they say they see is a *real world*—the very world they would have entered if they had died. All of this points with force to the reality of an afterlife in an afterworld.

We should not, however, assume that this world of light so often described by NDErs is the only world that awaits the dying. Not all NDEs are positive. In her book *Blessing in Disguise*, Dr. Barbara Rommer describes several dozen NDEs that are "less than positive." They range from a feeling of total emptiness in the tunnel to terrifying imagery. One man who failed at suicide encountered a huge ape he took to be Satan. Others felt condemned by an authority figure during their life review. But these experiences are relatively rare. Rommer says: "In over 300 interviews, the only time that an interviewee has felt judged by anyone but himself was in a Less-Than-Positive Near-Death Experience. Usually it was when suicide was either contemplated or attempted." She goes on to say that in these cases the authority figure "caused the experiencer to judge him or herself and instigate change." It is for this reason that she chose the title for her book.

NDEs do, however, leave in their wake puzzling questions. For one, some people who report NDE symptoms were not close to death. Some thought they were going to die—as in the case of a man whose car was skidding toward a bridge abutment, but came out of it unhurt. Apparently that fear was enough to catapult him out of his body; one researcher called this case a "fear-death experience." We also hear of fighter pilots going through high-G training in a giant spinning centrifuge having an out-of-body experience (OBE) after fainting, and subjects working in labs whose OBE was artificially induced by stimulating a region of the brain with a probe. Still others have had an NDE spontaneously for no assignable reason. I suspect that in most of these cases the experiencers really did leave their body. In the cases of the pilots in training, however, there was at best an experience of momentary exhilaration, but nothing remotely resembling a life-changing event.

Another puzzling feature of the NDE is the mix of imagery supplied by the experiencer's mind and the objective other-world environment. Dr. Melvin Morse, who did his research with children, tells of an eight-year-old girl in a diabetic coma who told him she saw a red and a green button; if she pressed the red one, she would go on; if the green, she would come back. Obviously she pressed the green one. I don't think for a second that the objective environment she found herself in while out of her body had such buttons, but that she projected them from her imagination or was shown them by a spirit guardian who created them for her, in both cases to help her make up her mind. The ape in the case discussed above had, I believe, a similar origin.

It's not without reason, therefore, that critics have claimed that since some of the features of the NDE are imagined, then the whole experience must be.

Such a conclusion, while admittedly perplexing, cannot account for the accurate reporting of distant events by NDErs lying comatose on a gurney, to take but one example. The fact that we have dreams does not require us to believe that our whole life is a dream.

An organization, the International Association for Near-Death Study (IANDS), is devoted to the study and analysis of the near-death experience. Thousands of NDEs are in their files, many of them published online for anyone to read. Dr. Bruce Greyson, former editor of the *Journal for Near-Death Studies*, is the dean of near-death study and is especially noted for his "Greyson Scale," a way of measuring the depth of an individual's NDE.

Today the University of Virginia Health System is the home of near-death study in America. Its bold sponsorship of near-death and other types of neurobehavioral research is unique in the academic world.

The work of IANDS and other research groups around the world give us, in the words of Dr. Larry Dossey, author of *One Mind*, "a very large nail in the coffin of materialism." Or, as I would put it, one more stick very difficult to break.

3.

APPARITIONS (GHOSTS)

Sometimes a student will ask me in the middle of class, "Professor Betty, do you believe in ghosts?" Such an undignified thing for a professor to admit to! But I do. I come right out and say, "Ghosts are part of our world. If you don't believe in them that's because you haven't personally met one or read the literature about them. The question to ask is not whether there are ghosts, but what is their nature." Having admitted this, I face half a dozen hands, and out come so many ghost stories that I have to put a stop to them! About half of Americans say they believe in ghosts.

Psychical researchers usually refer to ghosts as apparitions. Professor David Fontana, past president of the Society for Psychical Research and one of the world's leading psychical researchers before his death in 2010, defined an apparition as "something that registers upon the senses of an observer or observers, gives the impression of objective reality, yet isn't physically there." A special kind of apparition, referred to as a haunting, is seen repeatedly, usually by more than one person, and in only one place. Fontana believes that apparitions provide extremely strong evidence of an afterlife, as do I.

One of the most memorable ghost stories I ever heard was told to me by one of my colleagues, a math professor, brilliant, and, as you might expect, an incorrigible, hard-bitten atheist. He showed his contempt for religion and the Bible in face-to-face encounters in my office. I didn't look forward to his visits but tolerated them reasonably well.

Strange to say, he was married to a nurse, a devout Catholic and member of the Third Order of St. Francis, a lay organization demanding simplicity in dress, fasting, special prayers, works of charity, and other expressions of the Franciscan ideal. She was much younger than he, and he was devoted to her. When she died of breast cancer before she was 50, he was devastated.

The next time he came to my office was a few months after her death and he had a very different message, one that almost took my breath away:

> A few days after she died I was alone in the house and planning suicide. I was very intent on carrying it out, for I had nothing to live for. Suddenly—it was late afternoon and the lighting was dim—I looked up and saw my wife standing in front of me. She was surrounded by a soft golden light. And behind her stood a monk in a brown habit, really just his face under a brown cowl, sort of looking over her shoulder. I took him to be St. Francis. They both looked at me and didn't speak. Then they faded away. The whole thing didn't last more than five seconds. But it completely changed my life. I went from a man who scoffed at all talk of an afterlife to a man who hadn't the slightest doubt that my wife was still alive and had come back to save me from the deed I was contemplating. Oh, I can't prove to anyone what I now know to be true, but I know, I KNOW.

My eyes were moist when he finished. I let him know how amazing his story was and then dared to ask, "Did you by any chance think about becoming a Catholic?" "In haste!" he answered. "Without Carrie's appearance I would have killed myself. Life would have been unbearable. It's the church, her church, that has kept me reasonably sane."

He continued to drop by but now it was to show me how the Book of Genesis was consistent with all that science had to say about the universe's origins. It was just as pointless to argue with him about his extravagant theorizing as it had been earlier to argue about the existence of spirit! But I was happy for him.

The second ghost story is even more remarkable. I met Rachel at a local radio station where we and a few others were gathered to discuss some topic I don't even remember. But what Rachel told me as we waited to go on air I remember vividly and indelibly. Here is her somewhat edited account:

I was raised in the Assembly of God, a dogmatic Christian fundamentalist church. But now I believe in reincarnation, and I'll tell you why. I've never been regressed, and I don't remember a past life or anything like that. And I haven't converted to Hinduism or Buddhism. I don't even especially like the idea of reincarnation. Having to spend another life on earth is not for me if I can avoid it. And I don't like to think this isn't my first life. It means I must have screwed up in my previous ones.

But now I believe in it. Seven years ago I lost my baby sister Becky in a car crash. She was only nineteen at the time and loved life with a passion. It was an incredible tragedy for the family and everybody who knew her. Well, we put her in the ground two days later, and two days after that I got the key to her apartment and drove over to get her stuff out. At the time I was twenty-three and wasn't seeing anybody seriously. Well, I opened the door, and there, sitting on the sofa, was Becky. I just about fainted. I mean, every hair on my body stood straight out. I was totally freaked. "Becky, what are you doing here?!" I said. She looked real sad, just sitting calmly on the sofa and staring at me. She looked solid, not wispy like a ghost, but when I reached out to hug her she shook her head. There was something odd about the way she looked, like she shimmered a little or something. "What are you doing here?" I said more quietly. "You're dead. I mean . . ." Then she spoke. For five minutes we talked. It was the strangest conversation anybody ever had. I forgot to tell you Becky sort of believed in reincarnation when she was alive. This at first disturbed my mom, especially when she stopped going to church. Well, Becky told me she was real depressed and missed us terribly. She was definitely not ready to die and had never even thought about it. She loved life and all her things. Then she told me why she came back. She told me she wanted me to promise her something. She told me she wanted to come back as my baby girl when I got married. She made me promise to have a child as soon as I could. I wasn't even dating Rick at the time, but I never forgot my promise. And when we married, I got pregnant right away. And you ought to see my daughter now. We named her Rebecca, and she's four. And she's just like Becky! Her personality, even her expressions. And she loves cottage cheese, ate it sometimes instead of baby food. That's just like Becky, who was always eating it as part of her diet. Cottage cheese! Have you ever heard of a baby who liked cottage cheese? It's like, well, proof. I have no doubt they are the same person! . . .

I asked Rachel how she would answer if someone accused her of hallucinating her sister's ghost. She answered, "That would have been me before I saw one myself! I would tell the person I understood. I wouldn't expect him to believe me."

And skeptics do not, in fact, find themselves won over to a belief in survival by such stories. The math professor, they would say, was obviously distraught and could easily have imagined his wife's presence because life without her was unbearable; and the monk was nothing more than an imaginary verification of sorts. As for Rachel with her bizarre story of reincarnation, she could have been lying to attract my attention or been just plain crazy. Or perhaps her sister had imagined in the last moments of her life as her car hurdled down the cliff that she would come back again as her sister's baby, and her sister had somehow picked up on that memory telepathically and projected it into space, including the short conversation in the apartment. I mention this last possibility to show the extent nonbelievers will sometimes go to reduce the apparition to something they can live with—to something that does not require belief in "spirits" or an afterlife.

Nevertheless, the fact remains that the usual apparition is less than compelling from an evidential standpoint. The professor and Rachel both knew that the person they saw had died, and both were deeply attached to the person. So the possibility of an imagined phantom mimicking the deceased remains a possibility. A more compelling experience would be an apparition of someone who had died but was not known to have died, or was seen by someone not emotionally attached to the person, or was seen by several persons at the same time or in sequence, or conveyed information not known to the viewer or viewers that turned out to be true. There are many such apparitional accounts in the professional literature, and we'll look at two.

The first, a "collective sighting," is summarized by Fontana. Samuel Bull, a chimney sweep, died of what the English call "sooty cancer," leaving behind his invalid wife Jane, a married daughter, Mrs. Edwards, and several grandchildren, all living in the same house.

> In February 1932 Mrs. Edwards and her eldest child, a daughter Mary, aged 13, saw the apparition of Samuel Bull ascend the stairs and pass through a closed door into the room in which he had died, and which had been occupied by Mrs. Bull, who had nursed him faithfully during the years of his last illness. . . . Shortly afterwards, Mrs. Edwards and James Bull [Samuel's grandson] saw the apparition together. Hearing

of the sightings, Mrs. Bull confirmed that she had previously also seen it. Subsequently all the members of the family saw the apparition together on several occasions, all those present seeing it every time it appeared. Even the youngest child, a girl of about 5 years, recognized it as her grandfather.

Fontana goes on to say that the apparition looked "solid and lifelike, walking rather than gliding, and manifesting both in daylight and in artificial light. . . . Twice the apparition laid a hand, which felt cold, on Mrs. Bull's forehead, and once she heard him address her by name, Jane." After a while "the family became accustomed to the apparition," who seemed to take his place among the family once in a while.

Fontana thinks this case gives every evidence of Samuel Bull's apparition being the real, surviving Samuel Bull, though without a physical body. Here is his analysis:

> . . . where several people are involved and remain consistent in their stories, lying becomes less likely as an explanation, as do the possibilities that memory is playing tricks, or mistakes in observation may have been made. We are told that Samuel Bull's apparition was as solid as if he were alive, and that it was seen not only simultaneously by all family members present, but on one occasion remained intermittently visible for several hours. This is hardly the kind of occurrence that four adults and five children are all likely to mistake. It is also unlikely that both the Bulls and Edwardses, children included, were suffering psychotic episodes all at the same time....We can hardly suppose that all of them, including a five-year-old child, were projecting outwards exactly the same impressions of the dead man, and at exactly the same time.... Similarly it is difficult to understand how it can take apparently intelligent action [if it is nothing more than a collective hallucination]. We are told that Samuel Bull placed his hand on his wife's forehead and spoke her name, and, in two of the examples given earlier, we are told that the apparitions actually held conversations with the living.

I should mention that this case is one of 130 collective apparitions that G. N. M. Tyrell, one of the 20th century's most respected psychical researchers, identified. Even if this particular case is a fraud, an extremely unlikely possibility, the chance that all 130 are approaches zero.

The second case is an example in which the apparition gives verifiable information unknown to the viewer or viewers. Often such cases involve the apparition informing a friend of his death—as in the case we will summarize here. A British Army colonel awoke at dawn to find an old friend, Major Poole, standing by his bed. The colonel described in a letter what happened next:

> Standing by my bed, between me and the chest of drawers, I saw a figure, which in spite of the unwonted dress—unwonted, at least, to me—and of a full black beard, I at once recognized as that of my old brother-officer.... His face was pale, but his bright black eyes shone as keenly as when, a year and a half before, they had looked upon me as he stood with one foot on the hansom, bidding me adieu.

> Fully impressed for the brief moment that we were stationed together at C____ in Ireland or somewhere, and thinking I was in my barrack-room, I said "Hallo! P., am I late for parade?" P. looked at me steadily, and replied, "I'm shot."

> "Shot! I exclaimed. "Good God! How and where?"

> "Through the lungs," replied P., and as he spoke his right hand moved slowly up the breast, until the fingers rested over the right lung.

> "What were you doing?" I asked.

> "The General sent me forward," he answered, and the right hand left the breast to move slowly to the front, pointing over my head to the window, and at the same moment the figure melted away. I rubbed my eyes, to make sure I was not dreaming, and sprang out of bed.

Major P. was shot while storming a hilltop redoubt in South Africa during the Transvaal War in 1881. It is hard to imagine how a hallucinated phantom could accomplish what the colonel saw and heard. Carter explains:

> Two days later the colonel learned of his friend's death, at almost the exact time he had seen the apparition. Six months later he met an officer who was at the battle and learned that J. P. had died after being shot through the right lung, wearing the same uniform, and with a full beard, which the colonel "had never seen him wear." There seems to be no explanation for the beard if the image of the colonel's friend originated

only in the mind of the colonel, due to the telepathic perception of his friend's death. A skeptic of survival could, of course, maintain that the colonel clairvoyantly perceived his dead friend's appearance, but this would be postulating a level of telepathy and clairvoyance rarely, if ever, seen, apart from apparition cases such as this. It is also worth pointing out that the colonel had never had an experience like this before or since, and considered himself "not a believer in ghosts, spirit manifestations, or Esoteric Buddhism."

Stories like the four we have looked at here have come down to us from all societies. The Bible is full of apparitions. On one famous occasion the so-called Witch of Endor sees the spirit of the prophet Samuel "coming up from the earth" to tell King Saul he will be defeated and will die the next day. A thousand years later the Angel Gabriel appears to Zechariah to announce the birth of John the Baptist, and a few months later to Mary to tell her she will be the mother of Jesus. The Quran and the later Sayings of Muhammad report in many places that angels show themselves to mortals. The scriptures of India, China, and Japan abound in reports of meetings between humans and spirits. And in Africa stories of spirit epiphanies are part of almost every tribe's lore, right up to the present day.

How likely is it that all these reports across so many cultures and centuries, are, without exception, illusions? Even those apparitions seen by only one person, and without benefit of accurate information, are usually enough to convince the viewer that the apparition was a living spirit belonging to another realm who in most cases once lived as a mortal on earth. For such lucky viewers there is no need to honor the counter-arguments of skeptics and debunkers who deny an afterlife. Like the math professor, they KNOW. As David Fontana says, "We should not ignore this vast data bank of important human experience." Nevertheless, most of us of skeptical disposition need more than a few ghost stories to open our minds to an afterlife. We need good cases like the latter two examined here, and examined at much greater length in the technical reports written for professional researchers. Taken all together—the relatively rare cases of speaking apparitions providing correct information otherwise unknowable, other apparitions seen by several viewers in good lighting, and the great mass of ordinary "ghosts" seen by a single viewer—they provide another stick in support of an afterlife that is very difficult to break.

The continents of matter and spirit, still far apart, are moving toward each other and give hints of an eventual partnership, each respecting the other's domain and making room for it.

4.

POLTERGEIST PHENOMENA

The word *poltergeist* in German literally means a disorderly, disruptive, or noisy spirit (*geist*). Unlike apparitions, poltergeists are seldom seen; but the impact they have on their locale is not only seen but usually heard as well. Some psychical researchers think these disturbances are caused by a mysterious psychic discharge of energy from a living person, almost always someone in the house who resides there. If they are right, then the poltergeist is simply an inexplicable phenomenon, not a spirit or discarnate intelligence, and wouldn't serve as evidence of an afterlife. Others think the disturbances are caused by an unseen intelligence trying to convey a message—usually to the resident or residents of the house. In that case we can speak of a *geist* in the fullest sense of the word, an invisible person-like being, motivated to bring about change in the physical world. Still other researchers, probably the majority, think that some poltergeists are of the first type, and others of the second. Needless to say, if only *one* is a spirit, then the evidence of an afterlife for the rest of us is very strong. In fact the literature provides many instances of what appear to be spirits.

Rather than look at several cases, as we did in the previous chapters, we'll devote most of our time to investigating one in depth. I'm not a field researcher by trade, but in this case I became one. The case fell into my lap unsought; it took place about a mile from my office on campus. I was called to the scene because no one else in Bakersfield,

California, knew how to get help for the poltergeist's desperate victim. The editor of the *Journal of the Society for Psychical Research*, where it was published in 1984, was as struck by its evidential power as I was; from where I sit, it argues compellingly for a spirit source and therefore an afterlife. In addition, it's a bit of a thriller in the telling. Here it is, edited for a commercial audience:[1]

On January 27, 1982, a certain Paula Calvin called me and explained that a friend of hers was "in trouble." She described what appeared to me as a rather typical poltergeist outbreak (though she did not use the word) and asked me to help. I immediately called the "victim," a certain Frances Freeborn. Frances, sixty-three years old, turned out to be a wealthy, prominent, civic-minded widow and the executive director of an important non-profit organization in town. I would later learn that she did not drink, had never used drugs or smoked pot, and was not on medication. She had every reason to be embarrassed about what was happening to her, and told me so. She was somewhat impatient with my theories and only wanted to know if I could help "get rid of it, whatever it is." At my wit's end, but desiring to help, I called a friend, Ava Jacobs, a wise old soul who at the time knew more about these matters than I. Ava, her fifteen-year-old daughter Jennie (a gifted sensitive), and I converged on Frances' house that afternoon.

Frances' white single-story three-bedroom home is an attractively furnished, comfortable, but unpretentious dwelling in a middle class senior community known as Kern City. She paid for the house in cash and owned it fully. As you walk through the front door and stand in the living room, you might first notice the green expanse of a golf course through the sliding glass doors behind the dining room table. Off to the left is a hallway leading to the three bedrooms. Straight ahead is the kitchen, off to the right sharing a wall with the living room is the garage, and behind the garage looking out onto the golf course is the study. Even though the houses are built fairly close to each other, the neighborhood is quiet. Frances' most obvious neighbors are rabbits in her backyard, which her dog, Missie, a Yorkshire terrier, sometimes barks at. Frances had been living in the house for only two months when I arrived on the scene.

The other leading figure in this story is Mrs. Margaret ("Meg") Lyons (pseudonym). Meg lived in this house since 1962, when it was built. Her

---

[1] The full account can be accessed at http://csub.academia.edu/StaffordBetty.

husband died a few months after moving in. In the late 60s she married Bradley S. Lyons (pseudonym). Meg was a career woman with the Girl Scouts and was remembered by her son-in-law, Luke Cowley (pseudonym), whom I interviewed extensively, as "a dominating woman in a completely subtle way, very autonomous." Luke, who was close to his mother-in-law, described her as "clever, incredibly successful, great in groups, enjoying attention, always the focal point, extremely vibrant, scintillating, strong, very beautiful, the pocket-Venus type, stubborn as hell, tiny, only 4'11." In answer to questions I directed to him, Luke answered that Meg loved life, never discussed religious issues, had an "extremely formalized" religion, and was decidedly unready to die when death came quickly and unexpectedly at the age of 74. She loved the house; Luke remembers how visitors would sometimes exclaim, "This house is Meg!" She had always wanted her daughter, Johnella Cowley (pseudonym), Luke's wife, to live in it someday.

Meg died in December 1976. A few months later her widower, Bradley, moved out, and Luke, always hoping that Johnella would change her mind and consent to move to Bakersfield from their home in Petaluma, looked after the house intermittently for the next four-and-a-half years. Once every three weeks or so he would drive down from Petaluma and spend three days to a week in the house; usually he would come by himself, but on rare occasions his two sons or Johnella would come with him. Once in 1979 Johnella spent three weeks in the house by herself. But until Frances moved in on November 30, 1981, the house had no steady tenant.

My visit to Frances' house was undertaken out of a desire to help. I had no intention at the time of writing up a report, for nothing about the case struck me as especially exceptional; it was a standard poltergeist outbreak. When I was called in, I met Ava and Jennie, and we spent three hours in the house with Frances looking on. I assembled the facts from Frances and tested for normal explanations of the phenomena reported. Meanwhile Ava conferred with Jennie about what she "saw." Then followed the "the exorcism." I am not sensitive, neither is Frances; we merely looked on and mentally recorded our impressions of the goings-on of Ava and Jennie. Frances later told me that at the time she thought the exorcism was an "exercise in futility." She also confided that she had never placed much credibility in "psychic stuff," and that when she called her friend Paula on the morning of this visit, she had not asked for help from a parapsychologist. Paula, whose husband is a real estate agent, took it upon herself to call me and urged me to call

Frances and establish contact. Had Paula not called me, Frances would have put her house on the market, with Paula's husband as her agent, and this story would never have been told. The upshot of all this is that only by the most unlikely circumstance did Frances and I get together in the first place. Trickery or fraud of any kind was, for these and other reasons to be cited below, out of the question.

In the ensuing months after this first meeting, I all but forgot about the case. I still had no intention of reporting it and satisfied myself with referring to it in my parapsychology class in Spring 1982. Then, on December 9, 1982, I got a call from Frances, almost a year after the exorcism. She didn't tell me why she wanted to see me the next morning, but it was obvious she was very excited about something.

The next day I met Luke for the first time. Luke, you will recall, was Meg's son-in-law, and had looked after the house during its vacancy from 1977 through 1981. He was a retired career army man, an intelligent, skeptical, freethinking sort of person in his mid-sixties. He held a master's degree in English literature and at one time taught courses in literature at Ohio State and military history at the University of San Francisco. He had long been curious about psychic phenomena but had no known psychic abilities.

Frances had bought the house in November 1981 from Luke; it was then that they met for the first time. But their relationship was destined to continue beyond the business transaction. A week after moving in, Frances put in an emergency phone call to Luke in Petaluma. And then, a year later, the three of us found ourselves sitting together in Frances' living room. It was during this intensive seven-hour interview that I realized I had stumbled upon a case that was extraordinary. It became apparent then that the poltergeist had been active long before Frances moved in, and that therefore she was almost certainly not the generating force of the phenomena reported below. It also became increasingly apparent that the poltergeist, whatever its nature, was intelligent.

For reasons that will become clear below, the circumstances surrounding Frances' move into her new house must be reviewed. When Frances was first shown the house by her agent, it was in the condition that Meg had left it five years earlier. Her family pictures were still mounted on the walls, her furniture was in place, her clothes hung in the closet, even her underwear was folded in dresser drawers. But within a week, the house was completely transformed when Frances moved in. She brought in her own furniture; she put in new carpet throughout the house; most significantly she made two changes in the kitchen:

where a kitchen dinette set had been, she installed a long counter with a cabinet of sliding drawers and hinged doors underneath. She also put in a new sink, raised the counter on either side of the sink several inches (Frances was eight inches taller than Meg was and had back problems), and replaced the worn tile of the counter with a different colored formica. In these and many other ways Frances redefined the character of the house. Meg's blue rugs, gilt furniture, and colorful peacocks gave way to Frances' more subdued taste.

It had been nineteen months since Frances' husband had died. She had experienced the usual dislocations of acute grief while in her old house, but had not experienced anything paranormal. Her period of active grieving had long passed by the time of the move. She eagerly anticipated the move; she had no regrets about leaving her old house, which was too big.

Poltergeist phenomena began the day Frances moved in and continued for two months. I have grouped the reported activity under fifteen headings.

1. The actual moving of furniture was completed by about 10 p.m., November 30. The movers had just left and Frances was sitting quietly in her new living room. Suddenly she noticed a peculiar thumping and chafing noise coming from what seemed like the kitchen. She vaguely wondered what it was, but dismissed it as either heat expansion noises (the furnace was on) or the plug knocking and dragging against the cooler on the roof (this had happened once before in her previous house). Not in the least alarmed, she prepared for bed. As planned, she shut the doors leading into the two unused bedrooms and the unused bathroom; Luke had kept the vents leading into these rooms closed in order to save on heating expense, and Frances decided to follow Luke's example; she made a point of closing the doors to these rooms.

2. The next morning when Frances got up, she found these three doors wide open and thought to herself that there must be a draft in the house. That very day she called in a repairman, Ernest Dozier, and had him weatherstrip the front door and raise the stoop of the door leading out from the dining room into the garage. She later showed me the work that Dozier had done; he had raised the stoop approximately one-half inch. Both doors fit snugly.

3. That first morning the sewer system backed up while Frances was showering. That same day she called in plumbers, and they dug up the yard: the system was in a state of total disintegration. Frances

35

was very annoyed at having to spend $600 to repair the system, for the escrow papers indicated that the house was in perfect shape. A week later, after additional problems, Frances would place a call to Luke in Petaluma and stop just short of accusing him of a breach of contract. Luke assured her (and me) that during the years he had been using the house there had never been a problem with the drains.

4. On the day of the move (November 30) Luke offered Frances a pink vanity bench that had belonged to Meg. Frances said she would be glad to have it, and the bench was placed in front of the built-in dressing table in the master bedroom. For the next three or four days Frances kept finding the bench pulled out; always she would push it back in under the table, only to discover that it was out and 'in the way' a little later. She was sufficiently annoyed by the bench to store it in the garage on approximately her fourth day in the house. At the time, however, it did not occur to her that there was anything paranormally odd about the bench; it was not until she began to think in paranormal terms that she realized how unlikely it was that she herself would have left the bench pulled out so frequently. Of peripheral interest is the fact that when Luke's wife, Johnella, learned that he had given the bench away, she was upset. On his first trip to Bakersfield after Frances' move he managed to get the bench back, and Johnella began using the bench in her home in Petaluma. The gist of all this is that Meg had a great attachment to the bench, and that Johnella wanted it for sentimental purposes.

5. On her second night in the house, around 9.30, Frances was eating in the dining room when she again heard noises apparently coming from the kitchen. But still she was unsuspicious, and remembered wondering if a squirrel or even a bird could have come in through the roof vent to seek warmth.

6. That night Frances slept on a couch in her living room because her back was bothering her. As before, she made a point of closing doors. In addition to the three aforementioned, she closed the door to the master bedroom and the sliding door leading into the kitchen. The next morning all five of these doors were wide open. Furthermore, all of the sliding drawers of the newly installed cabinet were open (but not so far as to fall out), and the cabinet doors underneath the drawers were also open. Frances called Ernest Dozier back into the house, this time to check the door latches. He assured her the latches were working normally. (I, of course, later checked them myself, and they worked perfectly.) She also called in the carpenter who made the cabinet and

asked him to see if it was level. It was exactly level. Frances remembers the carpenter's quizzical look; it was only then, for the first time, that she asked herself, "What the hell's happening here?" Still, she dismissed it: perhaps she hadn't actually latched the doors, she thought, and vibrations from truck traffic on a highway a block away might have jostled the drawers and doors open. I later checked these drawers and doors for drag, and they were entirely normal; a strong earthquake, which hit Coalinga, ninety miles north of Bakersfield, on May 2, 1983, failed to budge them (Frances would later tell me) even though Bakersfield rocked and rolled.

7. For the next two months, on arising, Frances usually found the hallway doors open, the sliding kitchen door open, and the drawers under the counter open. On several occasions she experimented, opening the doors and drawers herself before going to bed; when she did this, they would usually be *closed* the next morning. "Five out of seven nights on the average something would happen," she reported.

8. Within the first week of Frances' moving in, the chain operating the motor-driven garage door snapped.

9. It wasn't long before the lights began acting up. When Frances came home, day or night, she found one of three lights—in the living room, in the dining room, or in the kitchen—turned on. Soon she called in an electrician and had each of the light switches replaced. The replacement of these switches seemed to solve the problem. But no sooner had this problem been solved than two more lights, one in each of the bathrooms, started to turn on by themselves when Frances was out of the house. When she replaced these switches, this particular disturbance again ceased. It was after the initial light episode—about a week after the move—that Frances called Luke in Petaluma. She tactfully complained about the light switches, the sewer, and the garage door. Luke reported that he was more surprised than Frances, for he knew the house well and there had never been any problems with any of them. Frances remembered Luke saying, "It's as if the house is complaining about you being there." But there was no discussion of paranormality.

10. Frances experienced the first violent poltergeist outbreak about two weeks after her move. She was wide awake, smoking a cigarette in the living room one afternoon, when suddenly the sliding kitchen door roared shut, and sounds came from the kitchen as if "half a dozen people were banging around." The sounds lasted no longer than might a rumble of thunder; when she entered the kitchen, she found the cabinet drawers and doors open, but there was no damage. It was

from that point on that she began to consider the possibility—"with half my mind," as she put it—that she was sharing her house with a spirit who was trying to provoke her. As yet, however, she felt no threat from whatever it was. "I felt it would do me no harm as long as I didn't cross it," she said.

11. Frances began noting her dog Missie's behavior. "She would be sound asleep, then she'd perk her ears up, run down the hall, scratch on the door, like someone was calling her; it was strange, queer; she never behaved like that before." At other times, Missie would rush across the room and cock her head back and forth, as if responding to someone calling her. (I witnessed this myself on the day of the exorcism). She had never done this before. Had it been a rabbit or some other animal outside, she would have run across the floor barking; Missie almost never barked at people.

12. Frances noticed by accident that it was clammy and cold in one corner of the living room. The cold extended out into the room no more than four feet. "You had to be right in the corner," she remembered. Luke later reported that Meg kept a large rubber tree in this corner.

13. About a month after moving in, Frances began hanging pictures. One of these was a brightly colored picture of three women stylishly dressed in pre-Civil War costumes; each woman was framed by an oval cut out of the background. Frances tried to hang this picture five times in five different places, but on each occasion the picture was, as it were, "taken down" from the wall overnight. The nail would still be in the wall, but the picture would be neatly propped up against the wall below where it had been hung, as if it had been placed there. After the fifth failure, Frances gave up the project for approximately ten days. She described what happened next:

> Then one day it was as if a presence directed me to pick up the picture and hang it on the wall of the second bedroom next to the light switch. I would never have hung it there myself. It was much too low and too close to the light switch, but I felt myself directed to hang it exactly there. It was like getting feedback from addressing an audience—you know how you sense an audience disagreeing with you or getting into it with you. That's how it was.

From that time forward the picture did not budge. When Frances showed it to me, I found it placed in a somewhat unlikely spot next to a light switch.

38

Shortly after Frances hung the picture successfully, Luke happened to be in Bakersfield visiting friends and dropped in to see Frances. (This was before the exorcism.) She was showing him around the house, and he noticed the picture. "I was shocked, stunned," he later told me. Meg had had a tri-oval picture very similar to it, though more subdued in color, and it had hung precisely in that spot. Luke later wondered if they were reproductions of the same print.

14. Frances began to feel a 'disagreeableness' when she fixed up the house, not every time, but often. "It was as if it—I called it it—disapproved of what I was doing." But as yet she sensed no danger from her "intruder."

15. On January 25, 1982, almost two months after her move, Frances experienced the most terrifying night of her life. It is highly significant that on this day she bought paint and wallpaper to redecorate the master bedroom (formerly Meg's and now Frances' bedroom), and moreover that she happened to set these down on the counter in the kitchen—the very counter that had replaced the dinette set where Meg had eaten, worked, and conversed with her husband or friends, and that Frances had installed when she moved in and that was the focus of most of the movement in the kitchen. All that evening she had the feeling of being observed; after she went to bed, she heard a ruckus in the kitchen. "It was like somebody was tearing the place up." But it stopped, and Frances, having heard this sort of commotion once before (see paragraph 10 above), stayed in bed and drifted off into an uneasy sleep. At 2 a.m. she got up to use the toilet. She did not turn on any lights; glare from the street lights and from the city across the golf course provided just enough light for her to see. I asked Frances to describe what followed, and here is her report:

> While washing my hands in the sink, the bathroom window slid back. I was startled and thought somebody was outside trying to break in. But I couldn't see anyone, and besides, the screen outside the window was in place. I pulled the window shut and, still not fully awake, yet alerted, went back into the bedroom, sat on the foot of the bed, and studied the bathroom wondering, "What in the world is happening?" About this time, the large bedroom window, which I always keep open even on the coldest nights, slammed shut, and the bathroom window opened again with a bang, both at the same time. I jumped to my feet. Almost immediately the activity shifted to the two closets on the other side of the room. At the exact time that the folding doors of one closet

opened, those of the other closed. This made quite a noise, and Missie was standing up on the foot of the bed, where she sleeps, turning her head back and forth from one closet to the other and yapping madly. Then I thought, "I've got to get out of here, this is just TOO MUCH"! With my heart racing I grabbed the dog and started for the hall. Though I had closed the door leading into the hall, as I always did, it was now open, and I charged through. But then I felt an impact; there was a zone of pressure, a mass out in the hall, as if something ominous and ugly was concentrated there. I stepped back into the frame of the doorway. Then I turned on the bedroom light (the switch was on the left) and looked to see who was there. Missie was yapping more shrilly than ever, but nothing visible was there. Then I realized that I had to get out of the house or I would die. But the hallway terrified me, and I wondered if I could break through the restricting force. I knew I had to give it a try, and I yelled loudly, "GET OUT OF MY WAY!" Then I charged through. I made contact with three entities. Two were on either side of me as I passed. I could literally feel them, just as one feels oneself brushed lightly in a crowd. I also knew that my passage in some way had caused them to disintegrate, to shatter, to lose power. They were startled and shocked that I had passed right through them. The third was directly in front of me but stepped back a little as I came through. It was appalled that I had passed through the other two. I can't say how I know this, only that I know.

When I got to the end of the hall, I realized I was only in my nightgown. I wasn't about to go back in the bedroom to get my robe, so I went to the closet and grabbed my London Fog coat. I started to open the front door, realized the garage was shut, and that anyway my purse with the keys was on one of the dining room chairs. So I ran across the living room (the coat still over my arm), grabbed my purse, opened the back door leading into the garage, hit the switch that opens the garage door and started the motor as the door slowly rose (it seemed like a thousand years!) I put the car into reverse and hit the gas so hard that I flew down the driveway clear across the street up over the curb into my neighbor's yard—the jolt going over the curb made me release the gas pedal. Then I pulled the car into gear and roared down the street, turned the corner and headed towards Bakersfield downtown. Suddenly I wondered where I was going and why this way? I pulled over to the curb, realized I was shivering, got out of the car—I was still barefoot in my nightgown—and put my coat on, then got back in and started the heater. I sat there for at least an hour, cried, cursed; I was as mad as I was terrified. Then I decided to drive to the Blue Moon Ranch [Frances' ranch] forty-two miles away because I couldn't see myself going to a motel looking like a wreck, with no shoes, and a nightgown hanging down below my coat. I remember that it was 4:25 when I got to the Ranch.

When I came home the next morning, I had fully resolved to SELL THE HOUSE, EVEN IF I HAD TO TAKE A LOSS. I just had to get out, this was intolerable. On entering the house I noticed a chill and a musty odor, like a dirt cellar or a swamp, a smell of decay. Then I noticed that the light in front of the coat closet had been turned off, so had the light in the bedroom, and the electric blanket. Then I saw why it was so cold—the bathroom window was still wide open. So was the garage door—I hadn't pressed the genie to close it when I left the night before.

In spite of all this, that afternoon Frances went to work as usual and called her friend Paula.

As described above, Paula called me. This was January 27, two days after Frances' terrifying experience. Ava, Jennie, and I arrived at Frances' house about the same time, 1:30 p.m.

At this point I must say a word about Ava and Jennie. Ava was a brilliant, multi-talented woman, a little over forty. She attended on scholarship and graduated from Scripps College, had since written several plays and a novel, and had a healing gift. I knew her very well. As for Jennie, she was as natural and uninhibited a teenager as any I have known. It is extremely unlikely that she faked what I witnessed; if there was any deliberate deception, it was she herself whom she deceived. Jennie "saw" spirits as easily and routinely as you and I see our coworkers. Her clairvoyant talents, coupled with her mother's gift of analysis, amateur knowledge of parapsychology, and overall sensitivity bordering on clairvoyance, were, I hoped, the allies I needed to help Frances.

It is worth noting Ava and Jennie's reaction as they entered the house. Each looked at the other and frowned: to them the place seemed "charged." Within minutes Jennie had 'seen,' not one spirit, but three—an older couple and a sad, lost young woman in her early twenties. Both Ava and Jennie agreed that the girl was probably not the poltergeist agent.

Ava and Jennie gravitated toward the bedroom next to the living room, with me trailing along; this room impressed them as peculiarly gloomy and oppressive. Meanwhile Frances was skeptical and rather disgusted with the queer procedure, and she sat in the living room and waited. Two things happened while we were in this bedroom that are worth noting. (1) Jennie's eyes followed the "movements" of the invisibles in the room. She was unaware that I was observing her—I said nothing to her about it at the time. (2) Frances suddenly screamed from the living room, "My God! What are you doing in there!" We left the bedroom at once and learned that Frances had just seen one of the dining room chairs, which had stood away from the table at a 45° angle, slowly turn and pull itself up against the table as if some invisible hand were "straightening up." I was privately skeptical and wondered if Frances had imagined it. But upon close investigation I noticed four clear indentations on the thick carpet where the rollers of the chair had apparently sat moments before.

The rest of the afternoon, an hour and a half, all four of us were together in the living room. Frances and I watched Jennie point to where the spirits were in the room, then watched as Ava tried to help the invisibles understand their unnatural condition. It's worth noting that both Ava and Jennie objected to the word "exorcism" as a description of what was accomplished. First, they said, they did not and would not force the spirits out of the house, and second, they were not concerned with "getting rid" of the spirits, with merely stopping the negative activity, but with healing and freeing them. I am using the term, however, because neither they nor I could think of a more precise one.

Ava's approach was both imaginative and rational. She proceeded in three-step fashion: (1) She began by getting the "spirits" relaxed: "Let's imagine them in an old fashioned porch swing right here [the entryway]," Ava told Jennie, and they invited the spirits to sit down, swing, and relax. (2) She tried to convince the spirits that *place* only existed for them because of their belief in it. She explained to them that if they thought in another way, they would find themselves on another "plane" altogether, one in which "place" was only a fiction. They seemed slow to catch on, however, and Ava worked ever so patiently with them. She tried to convince them that they *could* go, then a little later that they *should* go. But they hung back, afraid of the big world outside "their" home. Finally, waiting for the right moment, Ava declared that they *had* to go. And they did. Jennie saw them drift away, and, after searching the house for signs of them, Ava declared them to be gone. (3) Ava tried to convince Frances that the poltergeist effects she had experienced were impossible without subconscious "permission" and participation on her part. She suggested that in order to move objects, cause feelings, etc., Meg had to "borrow" energy from someone—in this case, Frances. Ava was completely unsuccessful, however, in persuading Frances of the existence, in herself, of any kind of "invitation," conscious or unconscious, for this kind of activity. Frances was in fact slightly offended.

A strange thing happened that night: absolutely nothing. There were no sounds, and even the doors stayed shut. "Well what do you know?" a surprised but still skeptical Frances thought to herself the next morning. For the next week she slept on the living room couch fully dressed, with the keys in the car and the garage door open; she kept her "flee zone" clear of obstacles just in case. She continued to live on edge, but she had decided to wait and see before she put the house up for sale. She did not have to. The poltergeist, whatever it was, had been neutralized, apparently by the exorcism. Five months later Frances painted and wallpapered the bedroom. There was no reprisal.

Luckily, the three adults I have worked with in this case are all intelligent, articulate, sane, and honest. Ava I already knew to be a person of integrity. Frances and Luke were strangers to me before the case, but long conversations with them have reassured me. I extensively interviewed Luke and Frances together and each individually, checking for contradictions in their accounts. There were none.

We are now in a position to weigh the evidence and come to a conclusion. First, can we be sure beyond all reasonable doubt that at least some of the phenomena are paranormal? Who or what is the poltergeist? The living Frances unconsciously "blowing off steam," or the deceased Meg and her team intelligently carrying out a plan?

Secondly, are there normal physical explanations which could satisfactorily account for the phenomena? For a number of them, yes. The sewer system, for example, probably backed up because on her first morning in the house Frances showered and used the washer simultaneously. Perhaps it had been years since the system had received such stress; in any case the plumbers reported the pipes were clogged with roots. The same kind of explanation can account for the broken garage-door, which after Frances moved in received unaccustomed use. We might also surmise that, since the light-switch episodes were neutralized by replacing the light switches, there was something faulty in the old light switches which made the lights come on by themselves— though this seems like a real stretch. One might also dismiss Frances' sensation of cold in the corner where Meg had kept the rubber tree, her sensations of disagreeableness, and her feeling that the house was malodorous on the day of her return after her night of terror. Reports of smells, not to mention supersensible gradations in psychological comfort, are too subtle and in general too "soft" for the scientist to trust, unless instruments are in use or a large number of people report the phenomena. But for the rest I find no normal explanation, unless we are to assume that Frances is a chronic hallucinator. But even this wildly implausible hypothesis fails to explain the "coincidence" of the pictures. Nor does it explain the indentations on the rug, left by the rotating chair on the day of the exorcism—indentations which I myself observed. Still less does it explain why Frances, who had no faith in Ava and Jennie's exorcism, stopped "hallucinating" after the exorcism. Nor does it explain why Frances, with no history at all of hallucination, should begin to hallucinate the day she moved into her new house, or why. If stress or trauma is presumed to be the cause, why didn't she hallucinate after her husband's unexpected death nineteen months earlier, etc.?

There is one other normal explanation that occurred to me: that Frances was a sleepwalker. Did Frances open the doors and drawers in her sleep? This is most unlikely. Aside from the implausibility of this explanation—no one had ever told her she walked in her sleep—it fails to account for the most striking phenomena, for Frances was awake throughout the violent episode when she fled the house. The only explanation that covers all the phenomena is a paranormal one. The most severe thumping and scraping and sliding noises in the kitchen, the almost nightly opening or closing of drawers and doors, the banging windows and closet doors in the bedroom on the climactic night, the five-times displaced picture, and the moving chair—especially when considered together—can be reasonably accounted for only by invoking a poltergeist as agent. Also, the strange reactions of the dog, the light-switch phenomena, the displaced vanity bench, and the cold spot in the house, though not by themselves decisive, give additional force to the poltergeist hypothesis. Finally, it is certainly possible that the broken garage door and plugged drain and Frances' "feelings of disagreeableness" and disapproval when she fixed up the house were poltergeist-related. It might be possible to account for three or four of the phenomena by a normal explanation, but it is unreasonable to the point of absurdity to try to account for all of them in this way.

These are the facts in a nutshell: Frances is an intelligent, stable, honest woman in her sixties with no history of, or special interest in, paranormal experience. For two months, in the winter of 1981-82, the house she had just moved into "went crazy," and there are no plausible, other than paranormal, explanations for all the phenomena she endured. Finally, many of the phenomena, paranormal or otherwise that are associated with the case, tantalizingly point to some connection with a person who died in 1976, Meg Lyons.

The question we want to answer is by now clear to everyone: Is the living Frances or the dead Meg the Kern City poltergeist?

I believe that an intelligent, self-determining, purposeful agency is demanded by the case we have explored; a random, unintended letting-off of steam emanating from Frances is inconsistent with the phenomena we've just examined for the following reasons:

1. A random force might have rattled doors, even smashed them in, but not turned doorknobs, as evidently happened night after night.

2. A random force might have rattled drawers, or, if sufficiently violent, propelled them out of their slots. But the cabinet drawers, though usually opened during the night, were never opened too far and as a result were never found on the floor.

3. The phenomena could and sometimes did occur when Frances was not in the house. The lights would often be turned on when she was out of the house; and occasionally the doors, which she always kept closed, would be opened too. Moreover, the shutting off of the lights and the electric blanket when (presumably) she was at the ranch point to an intelligent will, unless we assume that random energy is capable of a tidying-up tendency and can operate at a great distance.

4. The objects moved were selective. There were many lighter objects lying about the house which a random force may have moved before the ones "chosen." And there was not a single case of breakage of a dish or saucer or any other light object.

5. If a random force had been operative, the tri-oval picture targeted by the poltergeist (let us assume for the moment that a random force can have targets) would have been found in the morning sprawling on the floor at an angle and perhaps broken. Instead, on each of five occasions, it was found "propped up" on the floor,

neatly leaning against the wall immediately below the place it had been hung by Frances the previous day.

6. There was no tendency for objects close to Frances to move more frequently than objects far away from her. The picture was not in her bedroom, but in an adjoining bedroom; the first violent movement of objects in the kitchen occurred while she was fifteen feet away sitting in the living room, the second while she was twenty feet away in her bedroom. Only on the climactic night did objects near her move. If Frances herself were the agent, one would expect objects close to her to be more violently moved than objects farther away.

7. The renowned parapsychologist, Ian Stevenson, an expert in poltergeist cases, thought that an exorcism would have a much greater chance of working with a discarnate agent (in this case Meg) than with a living agent (Frances), especially one who, like Frances, was extremely skeptical of the entire bizarre procedure. The exorcism was indeed the 'therapy' which worked, but it is hard to imagine how it could have worked *with Frances*. Recall that she was very surprised the next morning when she found the doors still closed, and that she expected the poltergeist's return at any time.

8. Parapsychologists are eager to discover harrowing inner conflicts in living agents in order to explain why they of all people would manifest poltergeist activity. It is significant that Frances, during the two months duration of the poltergeist from December 1981 through January 1982, was experiencing no unusual stress, but that two or three months after the activity ceased she began to experience severe stress. She was pressured out of her job in August 1982 and suffered a heart attack in early September while travelling in China. Frances still rankles at the way she was forced to resign her position, yet during the intensely stressful summer of 1982 there was no poltergeist activity at all. Why not, if Frances was the agent?

9. For what it is worth, Frances insists that she was not the agent. If she were not so sensible a woman—she became a good friend after what we went through together and I got to know her

well—I would be unimpressed by this claim. Her explanation of how she knows she was not, is worth repeating: "I've been having headaches lately. A brain scan revealed nothing. Can you believe the doctor told me I probably bumped my head and that this was the cause? I told him I'd have known if I bumped my head that hard! This poltergeist is like that. I would know if I were the cause!"

I believe that the above nine points argue strongly for discarnate (spirit) agency. But we have not looked at the strongest evidence yet. What if we could make a good case, not only for discarnate agency, but for a *specific* discarnate agent? I believe that the latter case would reinforce the former. If I were a detective trying to solve a murder, and had good evidence that the murderer was a friend of the victim rather than a stranger, would not this evidence be greatly enhanced if additional evidence pointed to a specific friend? Let us now look at the evidence which in so many ways points to Meg, deceased in 1976, as the poltergeist agent. The most persuasive evidence of her agency can be gathered under two general headings.

(1) The poltergeist activity conforms, not to shifts in Frances' mental or emotional state, but to alterations in the house. The major alteration was, we might assume, Frances' living in the house. But was it? Perhaps the refurnishing of the house, the redesign of the kitchen, and the new paint and wallpaper would be more distressing to a discarnate homeowner than the appearance of a "'guest." (How does one speculate safely about such matters?) The first major structural alteration took place in the kitchen and was completed on the very day Frances moved in: workmen installed a bulky cabinet with a counter-top in the exact place where Meg's dinette set had been, put in a new kitchen sink and raised the space around it a few inches, and put in new formica. That very night the poltergeist disturbances began, and the locus of this first activity was the kitchen. For the next two months the kitchen would be the primary target of the activity. The opened drawers belonged to the new (offending?) cabinet; the kitchen door was usually opened during the night; and the two most rambunctious, noisy outbursts occurred in the kitchen, with the cabinet drawers and doors the specific targets. It's reasonable to assume that either Frances' moving in or her renovation of the house, especially the kitchen, triggered the activity. The disturbances began the very night that Frances with all her furniture moved in, and this move followed by only a few hours the structural alterations in the kitchen.

The link between the second violent outbreak and a potentially disruptive alteration in the house is just as easy to pinpoint. Recall that on the evening of January 25, 1982, shortly after Frances had gotten into bed, there was an uproar in the kitchen. Then, a few hours later, the climactic disturbance which Frances felt threatened her life occurred. It was earlier on this same day that Frances purchased paint and wallpaper with the intention of redecorating the master bedroom, the bedroom that had been Meg's. Moreover, Frances happened to place the paint, of all places, on top of the new counter in the kitchen. It is tempting to speculate that this double insult could not be tolerated by Meg and made her an implacable enemy determined to rid her home of the "intruder." This rather risky speculation becomes more plausible when we recall that Meg was attached to the house just as it was and wanted her daughter, Johnella, to move into it.

(2) Nevertheless, the above considerations by themselves might fail to convince a determined skeptic that Meg was the poltergeist. It is only when we combine them with what now follows that we are forced, in my opinion, to conclude with finality that Meg was the agent. I refer to the picture episode. The uniqueness of this case hangs on the coincidence that Meg and Frances happened fortuitously to have similar pictures. Two or three dozen pictures, mirrors, and various other hangings hung in Frances' house when I inspected it; Luke and Frances both reported that Meg hung many pictures, most of them family photographs, during her earthly tenure in the house. The fact that both women happened to hang two pictures which closely resembled each other was due to chance, but the fact that Frances hung her picture in precisely the same place in the house that Meg had hung hers could not be due to chance, especially when we recall Frances' five aborted attempts to hang the picture and then the mysterious guidance she felt as she hung the picture the sixth and final time. Everything about this episode suggests intelligent guidance. Considered along with all the other phenomena, it points almost irresistibly to Meg. We can claim with considerable confidence that Meg still existed discarnately, and that for a few years she continued to live in the house to which she in life was so attached. Just as the living who have formed deep attachments dislike change, so Meg disliked the changes that Frances was bringing about in the house. Defeated at every turn by the innovative and more powerful (because embodied) Frances, Meg scored her lone victory when she guided Frances' picture to its rightful place, and later nearly scored a decisive victory by almost driving Frances out of the house.

It's worth noting that Luke, as soon as he saw the picture, thought Meg was trying to send him a message. He felt she knew he would sooner or later visit and would recognize the picture in its place, in that way greeting him and letting him know she was still very much alive and thinking of him. I'm not convinced of Luke's reasoning and feel an equally plausible explanation is that Meg simply wanted the picture hung "in its rightful place." Either way, the "picture episode" argues convincingly for Meg as the poltergeist.

There are two less important evidences of Meg's agency that are worth mentioning. "Meg always kept the doors open; she liked the feeling of an open house," Luke recalled. This habit of hers in life would explain her open-door fetish in death. Secondly, we should not forget Luke's description of his mother-in-law as "a dominating woman ... stubborn as hell ... used to getting her way," and that she was unprepared to die. Perhaps she was unwilling to accept the usual consequences of death once it overtook her, and had the determination and the power to make an exception of herself, as an earthbound spirit, however unwise her decision might have been.

To conclude, I think the evidence presented here is best explained by postulating a self-determining, more-or-less intelligent discarnate agent, with links to a known deceased personality. Whether or not Meg was as fully competent as she was in the flesh is beyond the scope of this study; but there can be little doubt that the phenomena point to some kind of intelligent agent, probably the spirit of Meg Lyons, and that no living person's "blowing off steam" can even come close to accounting for all the phenomena.

The files held by the Society for Psychical Research and other parapsychology associations include many poltergeist cases. In recent years quite a few others have been caught on tape by surveillance cameras (CCTV). Someone even collected several of the best of these and placed them on YouTube.[2] The mysterious movements are similar to the case we've just looked at; especially noteworthy are the movements of furniture that give the appearance, not of random chaos, but of control by some invisible hand. At the very least they make it completely clear that poltergeists are part of our world.

Before leaving this subject, we will briefly survey a famous case from Cardiff, Wales. If you thought the Kern City poltergeist was strange, get ready for one even stranger. What makes it special is not only the

---

[2] https://www.youtube.com/watch?v=5s_BX38jiIo

49

remarkable range of the phenomena but that the investigator, David Fontana, past president of the Society for Psychical Research and one of the most renowned parapsychologists in the world in his day (he died in 2010), witnessed the phenomena first-hand, and on many occasions, over a two-year span (from June 1989 to early 1992).

The focus of the activity was a lawnmower repair shop and an adjoining garden-accessories shop. The poltergeist took apparent pleasure in the following activities, as reported by Fontana:[3]

1. The throwing of coins, bolts, and small stones the size of granite chippings (many of which were also found to litter the floor when John [Matthews, the owner,] opened the workshop in the morning, John at that time being the only one with the key) against the walls of the workshop.
2. The mysterious arrival of objects (termed "apports") of unknown origin such as a pen and keys.
3. Old pennies all dating from 1912 which either appeared to fall from the ceiling or which were found on the work surfaces.
4. Tools on racks set swinging with no apparent cause.
5. Blue flames emerging from a brass shell case which was kept as an ornament in the workshop and which was also sometimes "thrown" violently around the room.
6. Planks of wood apparently too heavy to be thrown by hand hurled from the yard through the open door of the workshop.
7. Stones thrown at Pat, John's wife, while she was in the toilet at the back of the workshop with the door locked.
8. Dust thrown down John's collar and that of a business associate who worked with him.
9. Loud knocks on the window of the shop when no one was visible outside.
10. Particularly frequent was the movement of small floats used in the carburetors of the lawnmowers under repair, of which there was a large stock in the workroom.

Fontana describes many events making use of the above material that suggests an intelligence engaged in play. So obvious was this to all involved—five respectable middle-aged people with a family or business connection to Matthews—that they gave the poltergeist a name, "Pete."

---

[3] Numbering added by me.

Pete especially enjoyed the "game" of "stone-throwing." Matthews discovered that if he threw the tiny stones at a corner of the store 20 feet away, stones would immediately fly back and hit the wall behind him. Fontana himself played the game:

> I tried my own hand at stone throwing, again from 20 feet away and aiming into the same corner of the workshop, and to my surprise a stone was returned, hitting the wall behind me. I tried again with the same result. Over the following days and weeks John, Pat, and I spent ... much time in the stone throwing game. Sometimes we got results, sometimes our stones were ignored. Nothing happened if we threw stones elsewhere in the workshop. Only the one corner, which we named the active corner, prompted a response.

> Now stones don't fly through rooms unless someone throws them. Still, the repetition of this single act over and over might suggest to the hard-core skeptic some sort of anomaly involving a physical force akin to a magnet. Far more difficult to explain are the following further disturbances. When "Pete" was asked to "bring" a certain tool from the workshop into the retail shop, the tool would invariably "arrive, seemingly falling from the ceiling and 'materializing' on the way down." Sometimes "Pete" didn't need to be asked. "For example, on unlocking the premises and entering the small kitchen that led off the workshop, John and Pat [John's wife] would sometimes find there had been rudimentary attempts to lay out cutlery on the table, as if for breakfast." On other occasions heavy or dangerous objects were "thrown," narrowly missing one of the occupants. It is especially interesting that amid all this "throwing" of objects, from tiny stones to a steel cylinder, no one was ever hurt. It seemed to all alike that "Pete" took great care not to harm anyone and had an uncanny knack to ensure it was so.

As for fraud, "I was extremely fortunate," Fontana reports, "in witnessing so many phenomena myself and in the company of individuals of whose integrity I had plenty of time and opportunity to satisfy myself." The case suggests personal agency in many ways, more than I've mentioned here. But who *was* the poltergeist? Paul, Pat's brother, saw the apparition of a boy on three occasions. Fontana reports that there was a local rumor that "a small boy had been killed in a traffic accident immediately nearby some years previously," a claim later vouched for by the boy's elder brother. But there was no way to prove the connection at the time, nor has any arrived since. So, unlike the Kern City poltergeist, we cannot say who the poltergeist was or what the motivation for all the activity was.

Nevertheless, it seems indisputable that "Pete" was an intelligent, purposeful, though disembodied being. Given that fact, it seems obvious that bodies are not required for personal life. If not, then what's true for "Pete" might well be true for us at some future date. When coupled to the Kern City poltergeist, along with hundreds more similar outbreaks in the literature, the case for survival of bodily death is greatly strengthened. One more stick has been added to the bundle.

5.

SPIRIT COMMUNICATION THROUGH MEDIUMS

Many of us who work closely with paranormal conscious states consider channeling, or communication by discarnate beings to our world through mediums, the most convincing evidence of life after death. Unfortunately, it also evokes the most suspicion from those unfamiliar with the best evidence.

There is no doubt that hucksters and frauds pretend to channel spirits for financial gain. The reason is obvious: How can you disprove their claims since no one can see the spirits even if they are really present? There is also evidence that certain mentally deranged individuals sincerely believe they are channeling spirits even when they almost certainly are not.

It is vitally important that we apply high standards when trying to determine which mediums—and which spirits—we can trust. When the best of them team up, they may be giving us information that can change the way we look at the world—not only our world, but the spirits'—and change it in a manner that gives ultimate meaning and hope to our lives. Or they may be giving us information about those loved ones who have died and now want to communicate with us. Needless to say, their messages can bring profound consolation to us when we are grieving.

Here is such a message. The channel is one of the world's greatest mediums of the last century, the Irish woman Geraldine Cummins. The spirit allegedly coming through her is Frederic Myers, one of the founders of the Society for Psychical Research. He has been dead for a little over 20 years when these communications begin. His primary interest is to persuade us there really is a world awaiting us when we die. His descriptions of that world—its appearance, its inhabitants, its laws—are fascinating and often exhilarating, as in the following:

> Within the subtle world of which I speak you will perceive a variety of forms which are not known on earth and therefore may not be expressed in words. Yet there is a certain similarity, a correspondence between the appearances on this luminiferous plane. Flowers are there; but these are in shapes unknown to you, exquisite in colour, radiant with light. Such colours, such lights are not contained within any earthly octave, are expressed by us in thoughts and not in words. For, as I previously remarked, words are for us obsolete. However, the soul, in this plane of consciousness, must struggle and labour, know sorrow but not earth sorrow, know ecstasy but not earth ecstasy. The sorrow is of a spiritual character, the ecstasy is of a spiritual kind.

This heightening of experience doesn't lead always to heavenly bliss, as Myers makes clear, but sometimes to intense suffering, as when one meets an old enemy. Myers tells us his hatred will hit "your body of light and colour" like a withering blast; for "the old emotional memory will awaken when you meet," and it will not be dimmed down by the sluggish earth brain you used to labor through. Myers explains further:

> You will understand, therefore, that pain and pleasure, joy and despair are once more experienced. Again, however, they differ greatly from the earthly conception of them; they are of a finer quality, of an intellectualised character. Mightier is their inspiration, more profound the despair they arouse, inconceivable the bliss they stir within the deeps of your being.

> On this luminiferous plane the struggle increases in intensity, the efforts expended are beyond the measure of earthly experience. But the results of such labour, of such intellectualised and spiritualised toil and battle also transcend the most superb emotion in the life of man. In brief, all experience is refined, heightened, intensified, and the actual zest of living is increased immeasurably.

I think most of us would agree that this is not a world we would want to miss. Myers needs almost 200 pages to describe his world and the worlds that lie beyond even him, which he has heard about from his teachers who reside there. Communications of this length are not unusual.

Bear in mind what channeling requires: the medium's mind suspends her own personality, moves over so to speak, and allows the spirit entry. Channeling is successful when the medium's thoughts and emotions are at rest and the spirit comes through clean and unbuffered. If the medium's mind "wakes up" and becomes active, her mind can reassert itself, and the spirit's message will be colored by the subconscious clutter, biases, and predispositions of the medium. The great mediums are those who are especially skilled at stilling their own minds and keeping them still. Cummins describes what it feels like:

> I am a mere listener, and through my stillness and passivity I lend my aid to the stranger who is speaking. It is hard to put such a psychological condition into words. I have the consciousness that my brain is being used by a stranger all the time. It is just as if an endless telegram is being tapped out on it. The great speed of the writing suggests actual dictation, as though some already prepared essay were being read out to my brain.... Whatever intelligence is operating, it may use my subconscious mind as an interpreter, may communicate in the language of thoughts or images and not of words.

Just as revealing is the process described by the communicating spirit. On his second visit to Cummins, Myers described (through her hand) how it worked:

> We communicate an impression through the inner mind of the medium. It receives the impression in a curious way. It has to contribute to the body of the message, we furnish the spirit of it. In other words, we send the thoughts and the words usually in which they must be framed, but the actual letters or spelling of the words are drawn from the medium's memory. Sometimes we only send the thoughts and the medium's unconscious mind clothes them in words.

The question now arises: How do we know that a spirit is really being channeled? How do we know the medium, even when we have every reason to trust her, isn't being deceived? The reasons are several.

Let's look more closely at Cummins. In her lifetime she channeled over fifty different spirits, and each had his or her own unique handwriting, none the same as hers. In addition, she wrote rapidly, so rapidly that someone had to "sit beside her in order to remove each sheet of paper as it is filled up." When one page was filled, her assistant lifted her hand and placed it at the top of the next page, "and the writing continues without a break." The skeptic could argue, however, that her unconscious mind is the real author. From what I have said so far, there is no way to prove it's not.

An earlier medium, the Anglican priest Stainton Moses, and one of the great English mediums of the late 19th century, makes a stronger case for spirit communication. Sometimes his conscious mind would be intent on reading a book while his hand would be writing "with unbroken regularity, [with] no fault in composition and often a sustained vigour and beauty of style." Even more interesting were the disputes that developed between himself and the spirit he was allegedly channeling, almost always over matters of religion. If *Spirit Teachings*, the record of writings that came through Moses' hand while he was in trance, is not what the title says they are, then it is at least very strange that his subconscious mind is at such odds with his conscious convictions. Nevertheless, the skeptic need only claim that such things are possible, and who are we to say they are not?

So we need still better evidence for claiming that spirits are behind these writings. The hunt for it leads to the concept of "evidential." *Evidential* is a term referring to information—correct information, *veridical* information—that comes from a medium who has no normal access to it, no way of knowing it, whereas the communicating spirit would be expected to know it.

Suppose you are sitting in the company of several others at a séance (or "sitting") conducted by a medium you have heard good things about. You have been "putting out a call" to your deceased father, whom you miss terribly, off and on all day; you hope the medium might put you in contact with him. You have made a point of telling no one that you will be attending the séance. You arrive incognito. The séance begins in the company of seven or eight others sitting around a table. After a centering process in which the medium tries to quiet her mind so spirits can come through her, she goes into a light trance; she feels she is receptive. At this point her spirit control announces that a man who claims he is the father of one of the sitters has shown up. (Mediums usually work with a spirit who acts as a kind of go-between or relay

56

on the Other Side—the so-called spirit control.) After a few minutes the control, using the medium's voice, reports that the man wants to speak to his daughter. You are excited and hopeful, but you are also dubious. How can you be sure it's your father who is coming through? This is where evidential becomes crucial.

Speaking through the medium's voice, the control asks if there is anyone present who might be this man's daughter. You immediately answer in the affirmative. The medium, or rather the control, relays the following: the spirit addresses you by the nickname he has always used for you, describes the games he played with you when you were a child, reminds you of a fall from a bicycle when you broke your wrist, mentions in passing the name of the pet dog the family loved, asks about your favorite uncle and aunt whom he names, and ensures you he is alive and well. These and other intimate details known only to you and your father are shared. He makes no mistakes. You are quite sure the medium had no way of knowing all this correct information. She didn't know you and didn't know you would be showing up at the séance. You are certain you have contacted your father. You are elated.

For most people that would be enough. But for psychical researchers it's not. That is because they fear that the medium might be reading your mind via telepathy. They need to rule out this possibility.

Some of the best cases in the annals of psychical research do just that. In one well known case involving the famous British medium Mrs. Gladys Osborne Leonard, she (or more precisely her control, allegedly relaying information from the spirit wishing to communicate, a certain Mr. Hugh Talbot) "began a tiresome description of a book" to his wife, who had no interest in the book and barely knew what the medium was referring to. On and on the medium went, describing the book's color and size, telling Mrs. Talbot she would find in it "a diagram of languages in the front . . . Indo-European, Aryan, Semitic languages and others," and that she must turn to pages 12 or 13 for something that would be especially relevant to their present conversation.

Could this really be her husband speaking, Mrs. Talbot wondered, or was the medium "tired and talking nonsense," as she suspected?

Mrs. Talbot went home, almost forgot about the book, but told the story to her sister and niece; both insisted she locate the book and examine its contents. She found it "at the back of a top bookshelf."

When she opened the book—it turned out to be a log book, a kind of diary—she was astounded. Inside the front cover was a "Table of Semitic or Syro-Arabian Languages" in her husband's handwriting, and on page 13 she found a passage transcribed from a book titled *Post Mortem* about survival of death.

There was only one person who knew what was in this book: her husband. Telepathy has been ruled out. Mr. Talbot apparently wanted to prove to his wife that he was alive and well, and he succeeded, even by the strictest standards.

This case was an early "book test." Other tests were arranged by spirits interested in proving their identity. For example, Stainton Moses, whom we met earlier in this chapter, received the following message from his control, Rector, who wrote through Moses' hand: "Go to the book case and take the last book but one on the second shelf, look at the last paragraph on page 94, and you will find this sentence. . . ." The sentence written out by Rector was found in Moses' library just as indicated. Thousands more of these book tests were devised by psychical researchers, mostly in Britain, over a thirty year period in the early twentieth century. Not all were successful, but the many successes were unaccountable by chance and ruled out telepathy for all but the most hardened skeptics.

Uncompromising skeptics are always on the lookout for a "slam dunk" that rules out telepathy once and for all, and even for them there are morsels of evidence that will test their capacity for obstinacy to the point of breaking. These are the ingenious puzzles devised by the deceased Frederic Myers to convince the world that he is alive. Unfortunately they are technical; the best involve a knowledge of classical Greek. My colleague Chris Carter devotes a whole chapter to them in his book *Science and the Afterlife Experience*, which I recommend highly.

Not all mediums work with words; some paint. The most celebrated is a Brazilian physician, Luiz Gasparetto. He claims to channel 40 deceased masters, from da Vinci to Picasso. He says that he feels their presence inside his body and sees them in spirit. How can we tell it's not him but them doing the painting? YouTube videos show him at work.

The evidence consists in the astonishing manner in which he works. We don't see the spirit masters, but we know from experience that no human painter can do what we see him doing. Artists themselves are particularly certain of this. We are left with an anomaly. Either we take Gasparetto's word for it, or we are left with no explanation at all.

He works rapidly, his hands almost a blur. His eyes are closed, his body weaving left and right, down and up. His hands work simultaneously, one painting in one corner of the canvas in one artist's style, the other in the center in another's. After five minutes both pictures are complete, each recognizably the work of the artist whose name Gasparetto signs. Staff writer Dick Roraback of *The Los Angeles Times* described what he saw on another occasion:

> As the man works, his eyes are tightly shut, his expression a tenuous alliance of grimace and grin.
>
> In precisely 1 minute and 35 seconds, the drawing is done. The man tosses the canvas to the floor, face down. He pauses just long enough to grab a second canvas, then sets to work again at an equally furious pace.
>
> Within 15 minutes, six canvases are produced: four in pastels; two in acrylics, the latter done without brushes, with bare hands and fists working paint dabs squeezed out of tubes.
>
> The first drawing is held up. It is recognizably Renoir. Then there is a Manet, a Toulouse-Lautrec, a Modigliani.... Later in the week there will be a Picasso, a Goya, a Van Gogh.
>
> An admirer asks him how he does it. "I don't do it," he says, "they do." Someone else asks him if it exhausts him. "No. It's pure joy. It's orgasmic," he replies.
>
> The Old Masters have been painting through him since he was 13.
>
> He has an explanation for it all: "It's all very logical. Why should God's most complex creatures just die? It doesn't make sense. And if they exist, why can't they communicate in some way?"

Gasparetto is not unique. His native Brazil has produced hundreds of psychic painters and even a few musicians. The country's most prolific author, Chico Xavier, wrote 450 spirit books while in trance; several of his most famous were novels set in the afterlife, ostensibly written by an author who was there and knew first-hand what he described. In a poll taken in Brazil in 2006, four years after his death, Xavier was elected "History's Greatest Brazilian," just ahead of Pele, the beloved Brazilian soccer player. He donated the royalties from his books to charity since, in his view, they were not really his; he lived always in modest circumstances. What Gasparetto made from the sale of his paintings went back into the free clinics he ran for Sao Paolo's destitute. Little wonder that Brazil is the Spiritist capital of the world.

Another especially noteworthy account of mediumship comes to us from Europe and is, as far as I know, the only successful attempt to play a game across the Great Divide. The game was chess.

The competitors were a living chess champion, Viktor Korchnoi, and a spirit communicator claiming to be the deceased Hungarian grandmaster Géza Maroczy. The match began in 1985.

The game was arranged by an amateur chess player, Dr. Wolfgang Eisenbeiss, who was looking for evidence of survival beyond death. The medium, Robert Rollans, did not know how to play chess and knew nothing about the history of the game, including the players involved. Rollans put out a call to the "Other Side" for any deceased grandmaster willing to challenge Korchnoi. "Maroczy" answered the call.

According to Michael Tymn, an expert on mediumship who has studied this case in depth,

> Before the game actually got underway, Maroczy expressed concerns about his ability to compete because he had gone so long without practice. "I was and will be at your disposal in this peculiar game of chess for two reasons," he communicated. "First because I also want to do something to aid mankind living on earth to become convinced that death does not end everything, but instead the mind is separated from the physical body and comes up in a new world, where individual life continues to manifest itself in a new unknown dimension." His second reason had to do with the glory of Hungary.

Because Korchnoi was often on the road and email was not yet available, the game lasted for over seven years. In the end Korchnoi was the victor. Parapsychologist Vernon Neppe, a former South African chess champion who analyzed all 48 moves, commented, "This level could not have been achieved by the medium even after great training, assuming the medium was not a chess genius."

But the communicator claiming to be Maroczy wasn't finished. Eisenbeiss and Korchnoi drew up a list of 81 questions about "the obscure life of Géza Maróczy," and Rollans relayed them to the spirit about a year after the match began. Over the next three years "Maroczy," using the medium Rollans' hand, wrote 38 pages of answers to these questions. Much of the information coming from him was so obscure that a professional historian was hired to check out the claims for accuracy.

Altogether "Maroczy" made 92 statements that required verification. The historian, after much trouble, was able to verify 85 as factual; the remaining seven couldn't be confirmed or disconfirmed.

Every good psychical researcher is on the lookout for fraud, and Tymn is no exception. He concluded:

> To chess experts the game alone offers convincing evidence that the discarnate Maroczy was in fact one of the players. But add in the personal and historical information communicated by the alleged Maroczy and the case appears to easily meet the "beyond a reasonable doubt" standard of our legal system and strongly suggests that personality survives physical death.

In our day most spirits speaking to us through mediums are concerned to bring comfort to the grief-stricken by sharing specific information that seemingly could be known only by the deceased, thereby proving their survival of death. This has always been the case, though in the heyday of psychical research spanning 50 years from about 1880 to 1930, many spirits had greater ambitions. They wanted to influence us, not by conducting book tests or painting pictures or playing chess, and not even by proving to their loved ones that they still existed through the use of evidential, but by describing their world, often in great detail. "A picture is worth a thousand words" seems to have been their strategy. Many people say they believe in an afterlife, but if they have no clear picture of it, if it remains vague, it's not of much help; it doesn't have the power to tame death, or, as William James famously said, to overpower "the skull grinning in at the banquet." Vivid, concrete, specific pictures have that power. The spirits knew that, and they provided those pictures usually through automatic writing, in which the spirit took over the hand of the medium and wrote out the script.

I've made something of a career reading these scripts, and I've always wondered if they came from the mediums' subconscious mind, in which case they would be nothing more than beguiling fiction. Over the years the impression made on me was that the accounts were too similar to each other to be fiction. If you've read thirty or more of them, and another one turns up on your desk, you can be pretty sure what's in it. They become repetitive, as you would expect if the same sort of place is being described over and over by different witnesses. This led me to believe that this "place" was probably not a figment of each individual medium's imagination. That "same sort of place" is what we call the afterlife, or, better still, the world of spirit. Early on in my research I was also struck by how the spirit communicators—most of whom had been Christians in earth life—departed from Christian doctrine once they died. They did so not in a spirit of rebellion, but because doctrines like the Trinity or the divinity of Jesus or his atoning death on the cross or salvation by faith alone—not to mention lesser doctrines like Jesus's virgin birth or his ascension into heaven—are never mentioned. Since most of the mediums were also Christian—many of them were Anglicans raised on the doctrines spelled out in the Nicene Creed—how could this be? You would expect Christian doctrine to appear almost routinely if the writings were nothing more than manifestations of the mediums' beliefs. A final reason for my taking seriously these communications as genuine revelations is their strange beauty. The best of them have always seemed to me utterances beyond human invention, as if coming from a higher world—like the most inspired music of Schubert or Brahms. (Brahms is famous for saying that "all truly inspired ideas come from God," not from the composer.) While writing my novel *The Imprisoned Splendor*, which is set in the afterlife and is based on my research, I struggled mightily with the settings. They transcended anything my unguided imagination could have produced on its own. For me this was a kind of confirmation that spirits were real and that one day I'd be one myself. I even wondered if I'd have a good laugh at some of the mistakes I made in the novel when too much of me got in the way of them. For what I got right, I owe to them—or so it seems.

In any case, here is a very short summary of the world they describe for us. (A fuller account can be found in my books *The Afterlife Unveiled* and *Heaven and Hell Unveiled*.)

1. The Afterworld is not some fantastic vision of infinity where souls are locked in poses of permanent rapture gazing at the face of God. And no one floats on a cloud while playing a harp. Rather it is a place with landscapes and seas and houses and cities reminiscent of our own world—a material world, but of higher vibration insensible to us earthlings. There are gardens, universities, libraries, and hospices for the newly dead—but no factories, fire stations, sanitary landfills, or smokestacks. There are no dirty jobs to do. "We have no traffic, and our roads are covered with the thickest and greenest grass, as soft to the feet as a bed of fresh moss. It is on these that we walk," says Msgr. Hugh Benson. All accounts describe a world of exquisite natural beauty.

2. The Afterworld begins at the earth's surface and extends outward. Earth is the nucleus of the entire world system that the spirits

describe. "The spirit world begins very near the earth and extends millions of miles beyond," writes Leslie Stringfellow. It "surrounds yours on all sides, like the atmosphere does the globe, and every nation has its counterpart in spirit, surrounding it, in connection with that part over or nearest its earthly place of residence."

3. Spirits do not usually refer to their world as heaven. Their world is actually a spectrum of realms stretching from the lowly joys and satisfactions of a novice soul just come over; to spheres of unimaginable radiance, perfection, and fulfillment that they have only heard about or at best visited; to darker, murkier regions where souls of a lower order reside.

4. The newly "dead" are thoroughly themselves when they pass. Their personalities and habits and character, for better or worse, are completely intact. Spirits are not omniscient. They don't get the answers to all the questions that puzzled them back on earth just because they've died. Many fail to grasp their condition; some, especially those who were certain that death meant extinction, even refuse to believe they have died. For, as we have seen, the landscapes of the astral world are similar to the landscapes of earth they left behind.

5. Though they are recognizably themselves, life in the astral is more vivid and intense than on earth, not more ghostly. Astral beings have fewer limitations. They can communicate telepathically and with much greater precision than through the cumbersome medium of speech. They can move from place to place by willing to be at their destination, though they can walk if they want to. Their minds are sharper, their emotions more acutely felt, both positive and negative. They see and hear as before, but in a more intense way. The old bodies they left behind do not follow them beyond death. Spirits are not naked, but clothed. Astral clothing is fashioned by the mind. There are no clothes closets in the astral.

6. The Afterworld is a broad-based society of every conceivable kind of person, most of them flawed and incomplete in some way or another. Many are no more motivated to "grow their souls" than they were back on earth. According to Judge Patterson-Hatch, "Most are content to assimilate the experiences they had on earth . . . most souls do not demand enough here, any more than they did in life." But the best are determined to advance.

7. Spirits are not allowed to overreach in the astral, but must grow in wisdom and in love gradually. They cannot enter a vibration or cross a boundary they are not ready for. There is justice in where they

end up at death. There is definitely a law of karma. They gravitate to their rightful place. They can move ahead only when they are changed enough to do so. Benson tells us, "Each sphere is completely invisible to the inhabitants of the spheres below it, and in this respect, at least, it provides its own boundary."

8. Many of them had ambitious plans for self-improvement before they descended into flesh, but the density of earth's matter, including their own dense brain, caused them to forget what they came for. Subject to material concepts, they lost their way. They died only to discover to their disappointment that they mostly failed to accomplish the goal they had set for themselves. But for many of them it's OK, for there has been much growth in unpremeditated ways.

9. The astral world provides opportunities for every wholesome interest or avocation - from science to music to theology to astral architecture to homebuilding. It is a joyful, endlessly fascinating place, full of challenges, for those who desire to grow.

10. Physical danger does not exist in the astral. Neither does physical illness. Eating is optional and sleep unnecessary. The calls of nature do not get even a mention.

11. Many astral inhabitants maintain a lively interest in the events of earth and long to help it progress. They claim that many or even most of earth's most brilliant achievements were inspired by spirits telepathically projecting their ideas. Nor do "the dead" forget their loved ones, whom they often seek to help with what we might call prayer in reverse.

12. Spirits do not meet an embodied personal God in the astral world. Instead many find themselves surrounded by an all-pervasive, penetrating Divine Light, full of understanding and love. This Light does not judge them, at least from the outside. They seem to judge themselves. As spirits advance, they move ever closer to the heart of the Creator.

13. They celebrate the presence of that Light in powerful rituals involving supremely grand music and displays of light, described in astonishing language. Music seems to be the supreme art of the astral, with most communicators noting its inspirational quality. According to Benson sound and light are coextensive: the astral is synesthetic. Painting, dance, theater, and architecture are also prominently mentioned. It is safe to say that the more refined a person's aesthetic taste is in this life, the more at home he or she will feel in the higher realms of the astral.

14. There are hellish regions in the astral, and large populations that make their home there. What is sometimes referred to as the Shadow

Lands is a vast world of many conditions. The landscapes vary from sordid city neighborhoods to parched, gray scrubland, to dark, lifeless deserts. The vivid clarity of higher realms is missing. Instead there is a dull overcast. Temporarily lost or confused or stubbornly unrepentant souls populate these regions. The Universe doesn't curtsy to bad behavior.

15. Missionary spirits minister to souls in the Shadow Lands. Residents can free themselves if they are willing to face up humbly to their errors and crimes and repent them. Some do; and most, perhaps all, will eventually. But many jeer at their would-be helpers and seem to prefer their dull lives over the challenges of higher worlds they are frightened of.

16. Some spirits tell us that no spirit remains forever in the dark regions. But God will never interfere with our free will. S/He will invite tirelessly, but will never force.

17. There are three basic ways to progress in the Afterworld: admitting defects in one's character, service to others, and yearning for higher states. Service to others demands effort, work, and sacrifice. Nowhere do the spirits describe a deity who requires us to flatter or glorify him with our prayers. That is not the way to progress.

18. There are no rigid creeds or magical beliefs that souls have to accept. Whether you are a Baptist or a Catholic or a Mormon or a Hindu or a Buddhist or a Muslim or an Anglican is of no importance. Many of earth's favorite religious dogmas are off the mark anyway, and the sooner they are recognized as such, the better.

19. There are no masks in the astral. You cannot hide from others what you are: the quality of light shining forth from your body tells all. Mattson tell us that our negative thoughts "go around like big, heavy, sluggish pieces of material – like mud or oil slicks." Even the house a spirit lives in reflects his spiritual stature. These facts can be humiliating at first, but it spurs spirits on to a greater effort to improve themselves.

20. Many accounts say that reincarnation is one of the keys to soul growth and is therefore crucial to the divine plan.

21. The Creator places souls in the difficult environment of earth because He (She) loves them. He wants to see them grow in wisdom, love, and power. He knows that the only way to bring out the best in a soul is to challenge it, in the same way that a good teacher challenges her students. Soul building, or character development, is the whole point of our sojourn, both on earth and beyond. The use we make of our free will is absolutely crucial to our progress at all levels. Meditation is one way we grow.

Other reasons for seeing mediumship as a powerful weapon against physicalism come from lab-based research. All over the world parapsychologists are studying extraordinary conscious states, from non-local awareness (telepathy and clairvoyance) to full-fledged mysticism. Much of it centers on mediums. It would take a long book just to begin to cover the topic, but I'll describe only one relevant finding. It comes from a neuroscientist, Andrew Newberg at Thomas Jefferson University in Philadelphia. An examination of his response to the findings would suggest, ironically, that he is a physicalist and nonbeliever in spirits.

Newberg worked with five experienced Brazilian mediums, all of them "adjusted and mentally healthy." While in trance the mediums' hands wrote automatically; the mediums had no idea what was being written through them. In their view they were the receptive instruments of spirits writing through them and nothing more. Utilizing brain scans and radioactive tracers, Newberg found that when the mediums' hands began to write, "parts of their brains involved in language and purposeful activity shut down." He was not surprised. But what he later found baffled him.

He discovered that the mediums produced "more complex language" when they went into trance. In his experience, the more complex the language, the more active the areas of the brain involved in "actively writing, concentrating and processing language." But this was not what happened. "In fact, it was just the opposite. The less active the brain was … the more complex the writing was."

In other words, the mediums' brains went dark when the writing they produced heated up. This makes no sense to a physicalist like Newberg. But to me it made perfect sense. If a spirit really is doing most of the work, then it follows that his partner, the medium, would have to do less. She doesn't think or plan or assess; she withdraws energy from the brain. She makes psychic space for the spirit to take over, and he utilizes no more of her brain than necessary. Remarkably, the writing becomes more complex than her usual writing. Someone else seems to be the author.

Many parapsychologists who have studied channeling at close range declare that the only explanation of the many different kinds of phenomena deriving from it make it all but certain that we survive death. Their voices ring out over the last century and a half. The famous naturalist and explorer Alfred Russel Wallace, co-originator with Darwin of the theory of natural selection, wrote over a hundred years ago:

The spiritual theory is the logical outcome of the whole of the facts. Those who deny it, in every instance with which I am acquainted, either from ignorance or disbelief, leave half the facts out of view. That theory is most scientific which best explains the whole series of phenomena; and I therefore claim that the spirit hypothesis is the most scientific, since even those who oppose it most strenuously often admit that it does explain all the facts, which cannot be said of any other hypothesis.

As for today, Chris Carter concludes that the best cases of medium-ship—however astonishing or bizarre or out of synch with what passes for established truth among physicalists—leave no doubt: "As others before me have concluded, survival of human consciousness past the point of biological death is a fact."

Our bundle of sticks keeps getting stouter and stronger.

6.

SPIRIT ATTACHMENT AND POSSESSION

Anew breed of therapist is healing the mentally ill not with talk and drug therapy, but by releasing troublesome or malevolent spirits—most of them human in a former physical life—who have attached themselves to their victims. I am not talking about religious healers like the Christian "deliverance minister" Francis McNutt, but secular healers, some of them licensed psychiatrists or psychologists, who have discovered, often by accident, that this new therapy works better than what they learned in medical or graduate school. They tell us that too often drug therapy only masks symptoms, and talk therapy reaches only as deep as the patient's conscious mind can go. But "spirit release" usually heals, often permanently. Not only does it heal the client; it heals the attached (or "possessing") spirit.

Dr. William Baldwin's *Spirit Releasement Therapy: A Technique Manual*, published in 1995, was a watershed event for this movement. Baldwin left a dentistry practice to pursue his passion. His ensuing Ph.D. dissertation in psychology was the first ever to take seriously spirit release—sometimes referred to as exorcism—as a legitimate therapy.

Baldwin, who died in 2004, and his disciples deal with spirits, or "entities" as they are often called, in a manner very different from most church-based exorcists and deliverance ministers. Missing is the adversarial command to "come out in the name of Jesus!" These alternative therapists treat the spirits with respect and compassion. To threaten anyone, living or dead, they say, only provokes an angry reaction; but a gentler, more rational approach is usually enough to coax the spirit out of its host and into the Light of the Afterworld, where it should have been all along. But not always.

Spirits come in several varieties, we are told. Most often they are EBs, or "earth bound." These are more attached to the loved ones they've left behind than to the Light they've turned their back on; others are addicted to earth's vices, such as alcohol or narcotics; still others are simply confused, not even sure they've died. But DFEs, or "dark force entities," are another matter. Intent on evildoing, they attach themselves to unsuspecting mortals to inflict maximum damage to self-esteem, family relations, and every expression of love. Speaking through their victims, they swear profusely. They are belligerent, disruptive, threatening, and thoroughly unpleasant. They might claim they belong to a Satanic Intelligence that rules them and punishes them when they fail at their tasks. Yet their loyalty to this Negative Force can be dislodged; with skillful handling, they, too, can be released into the Light.

One of the most extraordinary claims made by this new kind of healer is that nearly all of us, at one time or another, have had entities attached to us. How do they know? The same way they know everything else they tell us: Under hypnosis their clients, and the spirits speaking through them, *tell them.* Baldwin says he did not invent EBs and DFEs; they emerged, unsought, out of therapy sessions. Over and over and over. Other healers — like psychiatrists Shakuntala Modi, who practices in West Virginia, and Robert Alcorn in Ohio — describe a spiritual world and a method of dealing with it that follow in Baldwin's footsteps. One might suspect a conspiracy except for the fact that the movement is so widespread, with practitioners ranging from Hindu babas living in Pune, India, to a Polish healer who describes herself as a "therapist for ghosts as well as people, both needing the same love and care."

Most of us have a child or relative or friend whose life is shattered by depression, sexual dysphoria, obsessive compulsive disorder, eating disorder, chronic fatigue syndrome, schizophrenia, bipolar disorder, autism, or a host of other ailments. What if you were told that there was a healer who could get to the bottom of the problem and heal it, but that the source of the problem was probably an attached spirit? Would you go for it? Could you open your mind to the possibility that your sister's untreatable thirty-year-long bulimia could be stopped dead in its tracks by identifying the spirit behind the disease, releasing it into the Light, and then teaching her how to protect against a future attachment? All in this movement hope that you would. Dr. Alcorn writes:

> My patients are completely unaware of the presence of these others and therefore they have no conception of the problem or how to deal with it. The spirits who are attached pull them this way and that, throw them into a panic, destabilize their mood regulation, drain their energies, cloud their awareness and leave them searching for answers in the dark.

Healers like Alcorn regard their procedures, not as a throwback to medieval times when demoniacs were put to death, but as an advance. Dr. William Woolger, an internationally renowned transpersonal psychologist, sees them as "the next and essential stage in the development of psychology, a kind of return to the source."

In the meantime, Dr. Modi, the West Virginia psychiatrist, recommends a "protection prayer" for her patients, to be repeated every night. It begins, "I pray to God to please cleanse, heal, shield, illuminate, and protect me, all my family, friends . . ." And Dr. Louise Ireland-Frey devotes the last chapter of her book *Freeing the Captives* to techniques that victims of spirit attachment can use to *free themselves* from the invisible intruders. Some of them obsessively cling to their victims—often without any intention of harming them. What then? Ireland-Frey describes the technique used by three of her colleagues. Annabel Chaplin's advice for how to help a loved one who has died but is earthbound is instructive:

> Find a quiet place in your home...a time when you...will be reasonably certain of quiet.... Relax....Breathe in and out rhythmically....Your favorite prayer will help....Silently or vocally call the person by name....Now begin your conversation. Tell the person the reason for your trying to communicate...[and] the circumstance of the death. Very often the dead are not aware that they have passed on, and so it is important that they be told. Be very explicit. Remain calm and don't expect answers....If you have been unusually distressed, nervous, sleepless or ill since the demise, then say so, and emphasize that their presence is harming you. Reassure your loved ones that they will be looked after when they finally depart from the material world, and will benefit by the release. Last of all tell the departed to look for the guiding Light,

for helpers, relatives or friends who have gone on before. Give a final
word of love or blessing....Repeat, if necessary, the entire process several
times for about three days.

It's impossible not to be impressed by the successes of these "gen-
tle exorcists."

If these healers are correct in their claims, then obviously most,
maybe all, of the spirits attaching themselves to us have survived
death, and we have another stick to add to the bundle. But not so fast.
There can be no doubt that many clients have been helped by rituals
of depossession, spirit release, or exorcism (whichever term you prefer), but appearances can deceive. Materialists claim that when they
work, it's only because the client believes they work. That belief is the
engine that drives the client to health, not some spirit who has headed
for the exit! Dr. Modi herself confesses that she isn't completely certain
spirits are real—perhaps they are fantastic inventions made up out of
her patients' subconscious minds. Nevertheless, she, and all her colleagues, strongly suspect they *are* real. In what follows we'll see why.
But first a little history.

A great deal of Jesus' ministry was devoted to exorcising "evil spirits" or "demons." Seven specific accounts in the Synoptic Gospels (Matthew, Mark, Luke) show him casting them out of their human victims.
And St. Paul wrote to the early Christian community in Ephesus that
their struggle was not so much against worldly powers but "the spiritual
army of evil in the heavens." All over the Developing World right down
to the present day, "spirits," both good and bad, are taken for granted
as realities that share our world and sometimes must be dealt with.
Depossession rituals are commonplace throughout South and South-
east Asia, Central and South America, and sub-Saharan Africa; and
there is no place in the world where they are unknown. In the United
States, according to Catholic theologian Malachi Martin, there was "a
750 percent increase in the number of Exorcisms performed between
the early 1960s and the mid-1970s." And in England, according to Dom
Robert Petitpierre, editor of the Anglican "Exeter Report" on exorcism,
"incidents of demonic interference . . . since 1960 have become 'virtually an explosion.'" Yet most college graduates in the West—the smart
set as I like to call them—think that "spirits," at least the kind that oppress or possess us, are not real. Indeed the very raising of the question,
"Do evil spirits molest us?" seems to most of them like a return to the
Dark Ages and might be greeted with derision. In a dreamlike state of

delirium the agnostic Ivan, in Dostoevsky's *The Brothers Karamazov*, yells at the devil, "No, you are not someone apart, you are myself, you are I and nothing more! You are rubbish, you are my fancy." Doesn't Ivan speak for most of us today?

Yet there is mounting evidence that evil spirits are real and that they oppress and occasionally even possess the unwary, the weak, the unprepared, the unlucky, or the targeted.

Before proceeding, let me clarify both what I mean and do not mean by "evil" or "demonic spirits." I don't mean anything like devils with tails and pitchforks who fell from heaven with Lucifer and have been cursed by God to an eternal life in some cosmic ghetto, from where they tempt us to a similar perdition under the leadership of a head devil named Satan; none of what I say here is based on Christian or any other theology or mythology, though I appreciate their confirmation when it appears. By "evil spirits" I mean more or less intelligent beings, insensible to us, with a will of their own who seem to bother or oppress us or, in rare cases, possess our bodies outright, and with whom we can relate in a variety of ways. Most of them appear to have lived on earth as human beings and therefore to have survived death. In what follows we'll survey and assess some of this evidence, then suggest what psychiatry's reaction to it should be.

In 1924, Dr. Carl Wickland, a psychiatrist practicing in Los Angeles, published *30 Years Among the Dead*, a unique record of verbatim conversations he had with departed spirits using his wife as medium. Wickland divided his book into chapters based on what kind of spirit spoke through his wife. Some, both before and after their deaths, tormented women; others had been criminals, still others suicides. One chapter is devoted to spirits who were alcoholics during earth life and continued, after death, to "drink" through their victims. In one case Wickland talks to a spirit who has been parasitically using the body of a woman named "Mrs. V" to drink. Wickland uses electric shock to dislodge the spirit, then transfers the spirit to his wife's body, a trained Spiritualist medium. Once inside his wife's body, the spirit is addressed by Wickland, who tries to persuade the spirit to leave. Eventually he succeeds in making the spirit understand who he is, that he has died, that he is ruining a woman's life, and that he can get help for himself. As the session ends, the spirit, guided by his deceased mother, departs. Wickland closes the account with these words: "After the foregoing experience a friend reported a marked change for the better in Mrs. V., saying that no further desire for intoxicants was manifested. Mrs.

V. herself acknowledged this change and expressed her gratitude for the relief obtained."

Unfortunately, most spirits are not as obliging as Mrs. V's. When they are treated rudely or violently, as they are by many traditional exorcists all over the world, they often make a spectacle of themselves. India is typical.

A spirit healer in Western India is called a *baba* ("father," "holy man"), as is the god he works with and who gives him power to heal. (I will use the term here to refer exclusively to the human healer.) The way it works is this. A person who is deranged—we in the West would use words like severely depressed, manic-depressive, schizophrenic, or psychotic—is brought to the healer by her family. As she approaches the temple, she usually becomes visibly agitated. Or rather the earthbound spirit, called a *bhut* ("ghost"), within her does. Once the healing ritual is underway, the body of the victim becomes completely possessed by the tormenting *bhut*. At the climax of the ritual, the *baba* waves a tray of lights (*arati*) in front of each of the victims. These lights embody the power of the *baba* and the sponsoring god, and there is apparently nothing so agitating to a *bhut*. The body of the person may fall into a cataleptic trance, or moan and shake, or bash its head against a wall, or exhibit bizarre gyrations of supernatural force. John M. Stanley interviewed many spirit victims in the 1970s at a healing center in Pune after their recovery and found that none had been aware of any pain: ". . . all of the writhing and all of the agonies are experienced only by the *bhut*. The person himself, entirely unconscious, feels nothing." He also discovered that most of the afflicted persons who came regularly to the sessions—*bhuts* do not usually depart for good until they have been subjected to repeated exorcisms—were completely restored to normalcy.

Moving on to China, the Russian Daoist, Peter Goullart, presents a horrifying account of the last day of a three-day Daoist exorcism that he observed at a monastery near Shanghai in the 1920's. We are told what happened when a young farmer with "a wild, roving look in his fevered eyes" was approached by a Daoist abbot holding "an elongated ivory tablet, the symbol of wisdom and authority." The abbot commanded the spirits—for there were two—to come out of the man in the name of Shang Ti, the supreme Daoist Godhead. The spirits cursed the abbot "out of the energumen's distorted mouth in a strange, shrill voice, which sounded mechanical, inhuman—as if pronounced by a parrot." Then the havoc began. "With unutterable horror, we saw that [the man's body] began to swell visibly. On and on the dreadful process continued until he became a grotesque balloon of a man." Then, as the abbot concentrated and commanded more fiercely, "streams of malodorous excreta and effluvia flowed on to the ground in incredible profusion." This process, accompanied by an appalling stench, continued for an hour until the man finally resumed normal size. But the spirits were not finished:

> Another scene of horror evolved itself before our dazed eyes. The man on the bed became rigid and his muscles seemed to contract, turning him into a figure of stone. Slowly, very slowly, the iron bedstead, as if impelled by an enormous weight, caved in, its middle touching the ground. The attendants seized the inert man by his feet and arms. The weight was such that none of them could lift him up and they asked for assistance from the onlookers. Seven men could hardly lift him for he was heavy as a cast-iron statue.

Eventually, and suddenly, the man regained his normal weight. Then began the final struggle, abbot against spirits. As the abbot enlisted the help of Shang Ti (the "Supreme Power") and yelled "Get out! Get out!" the onlookers saw the victim's body convulse, his fingers claw his body until it was covered with blood, his eyes roll up under his skull, and then the final twisting paroxysm as the spirits came out of him with a wild scream, "Damn you! Damn you! We are going but you shall pay for it with your life." Suddenly, the man resumed his normal personality and asked where he was. He had no memory of anything that had happened. The exorcist was completely exhausted and had to be helped away.

Back in the States, Malachi Martin, Catholic theologian and former professor at the Vatican's Pontifical Biblical Institute, published in 1976 *Hostage to the Devil: The Possession and Exorcism of Five Americans*. At the time it was—and perhaps still is—the most convincing and authoritative book available on the subject. It was praised by the *New York Times Book Review, the Washington Post Book Review, Newsweek,* the *Psychology Today Book Club,* and a host of other prominent publications when it first appeared. We'll come back to it below. Then in 1983, M. Scott Peck, a Harvard-educated psychiatrist and author of the hugely popular self-help book *The Road Less Traveled,* startled the psychiatric community by describing his participation in two exorcisms. Peck says he personally confronted a profoundly evil spirit on both occasions.

In a number of ways these Christian exorcisms remind me of the Chinese account above. The demons reveal themselves to be utterly and horrifyingly malevolent; they cling to their victims with unbelievable tenacity and exhibit superhuman strength; and the exorcism requires a lot of time, often several days, to complete. Furthermore, the demons are expelled only after divine assistance is called on repeatedly, and the entire ordeal is exhausting to the exorcist and his team.

Peck tells us that the two patients he observed "were gravely ill from a psychiatric standpoint before their exorcisms," yet that after the exorcisms the mental state of these patients was dramatically improved. As one of the victims put it, "Before, the voices were in control of me; now I'm in control of the voices" Following additional psychotherapy, the voices died out and both patients made a full recovery.

"Genuine possession, as far as we know," writes Peck, "is very rare." "We should use the word possession only when it fits—for the rare Charles Manson's of the world," writes Francis MacNutt, a former Catholic priest and leading authority on possession. In MacNutt's experience most people under the influence of evil spirits are merely "oppressed" by demons—he likes the word "demonized"—but not completely possessed. And for these, exorcism is neither necessary nor desirable. Rather, such victims need "deliverance." Furthermore, the "true demons from hell," the kind that usually require a full-scale exorcism, "represent a relatively small percentage" of all the spirits capable of influencing us, says MacNutt, "perhaps only ten percent."

MacNutt believes that many mentally ill people—both within and outside of mental institutions—are oppressed by spirits. These spirits range from the truly Satanic to the "dead who are not at rest." These latter are not so much evil as confused. Yet in their blind selfishness these "earthbound spirits" can do serious, if unintended, harm. In relation to us, therefore, they are "evil."

What happens when an oppressing spirit or spirits are being delivered from a victim? MacNutt summarizes the signs under three headings: "bodily contortions, changes in the voice, and changes in facial expression." MacNutt's generalizations are reminiscent of the Asian cases we looked at above. Spirit victims sometimes show supernatural agility or strength. They "may arch their spines backward, while still others roll on the ground." Unnatural and unseemly bodily postures and motions are commonplace. Furthermore, "the tone of the person's voice changes. A woman may start speaking in a husky voice like a man, or a mild-mannered person may begin speaking in a snide, insulting tone of voice." Often the voice uses the plural *we*, and on rare occasions a foreign language, a language unknown to the victim, is spoken. As for changes in facial expression, MacNutt writes:

> Perhaps the most common external indication of demonization comes when the person's facial expression changes. It is as if you are no longer looking at the same person you started talking to. The old saying "The eyes are the windows of the soul" becomes especially meaningful. It is as if the evil spirit is peering out at you. The eyes become filled with hate, mockery, pride or whatever the nature of that particular spirit is. Now that the evil spirit has surfaced, you are no longer directly in touch with the person you have been praying for.

Other predictable features include rolling eyes, screams, gagging, fetid smells, and a feeling of cold in the room. (Several horrifying examples of possession are online through YouTube.) Finally, near the climax of the deliverance it is not uncommon, reports MacNutt, for the threatened spirit to temporarily possess the victim, as we saw in the Indian cases. When that happens:

> She probably will remember nothing she said or did during that time. She may have been shouting curses at you, or thrashing around and screaming, but afterward, mercifully, she will have no memory of it at all. In the end she will probably feel refreshed and ready for a celebration, while you and your team will feel exhausted and ready to sleep on the spot!

I haven't looked in depth at cases of possession from Africa or South or Central America, where they are frequently reported. The above cases, however, should be adequate for the preliminary form of evaluation needed here.

What do we do with all this evidence of apparent spirit oppression? In particular, can it be squared with the materialist worldview of Western psychiatry? Is "spirit oppression" always to be placed within quotation marks, or can we leave them off? Are "spirits" the hallucinations of a sick brain, or do they have an independent existence? I think every reader must grant, however grudgingly, that *on the surface* the phenomena point to dualist metaphysics: we are one kind of being, and spirits are another. We are visible, and they are not. We are subject to the laws of physics, and they are not. We have physical bodies, and they do not.

Yet they are as conscious as we are, as individual as we are. And most of them claim to have lived on earth at one time.

But what do we find when we look *below the surface?* Can materialist metaphysics be salvaged in the face of all this evidence? Can it be salvaged without sounding farfetched and perhaps ridiculous? More importantly, should psychiatry make room for, or even embrace, the "spiritual" therapies used in the above cases? Should it place them alongside the brain-altering drugs and electroconvulsive therapies (ECT) presently used? Should it learn to accept them as alternative therapies – just as medical science learned a generation ago to accept chiropractic treatment? Or are there good reasons for maintaining the status quo, as most materialists are determined to do? Is some form of dualism less of a stretch than materialism, or is it the other way round?

The following line of reasoning seems to me fruitful and suggestive. I'll evaluate the evidence under four headings;

1. Experience of the victim. Let's begin with an argument from introspection. A spirit victim, now healed, tells us he made intimate contact with an invisible, intelligent, malevolent "something" that seemed completely alien to him. "Solemnly and of my own free will, I wish to acknowledge that knowingly and freely I entered into possession by an evil spirit," wrote one of Malachi Martin's five possessed persons some months after his successful exorcism. Is it proper to dismiss such a confession as having no possible validity? Are any of us in a better position to speak with authority about some of the most mysterious "facts" of our own experience? When we assure ourselves that we have free will (to take an example from philosophy), do we finally have any convincing evidence? Determinists don't think we do. Yet almost all of us believe in free will implicitly and live by that belief. Why? Because our direct experience speaks with an authority that silences all arguments. In a similar manner the direct experience of victims of possession points with equal psychological force to the reality of spirits.

2. Universality. If spirit oppression were unique to one culture, religion, or geographical region, it would be suspect. Why would bothersome or evil spirits "pick on" only one kind of people? The fact that they do not discriminate, that their passions and machinations are as prevalent in India and China as in the Christian (or post-Christian) West, that they work their mischief all over the world makes us take them more seriously. What are taken to be spirits behave in the same way whether they oppress Americans or Chinese or Indians. They cause the victim's voice, face, and movements to change dramatically. They

feel just as threatened by a Daoist priest holding an ivory tablet as a Catholic priest holding a crucifix or an Indian *baba* waving a tray of lights. They are put to rout not by human agency acting alone, but by divine power, whether by Shang Ti or by an avatar of Krishna or by Jesus.

3. Unnatural or Superhuman Phenomena. When we read Goullart's account of the Daoist abbot exorcising the demons from the Chinese farmer, what do we make of the symptoms of possession? We see a man who blows up like a balloon, exudes a pool of excreta from his pores as he deflates, becomes as rigid and heavy as a cast-iron statue, caves in an iron bedstead while remaining motionless, resists being lifted by seven men, and writhes like a mortally wounded snake at the moment of release. Concerned to open the minds of his readers to the possibility of spirit possession, Huston Smith quotes this case in its entirety because, as he puts it, "it will be useful to have an example to show that there are cases that almost require it." Almost as remarkable are the uncanny movements of spirit victims undergoing exorcism at the hands of the Indian *baba*.

The question before us is this: Is it easier to believe human beings can do such things on their own with their bodies and minds, or that these things are unnatural and/or extra-human and can be done only by something alien to them *using* their bodies? If you observed first-hand someone in your own family inflate before your eyes and then speak a language you know he has never learned, in a voice that is not his, would you be more likely to conclude that he was showing an up-until-now unknown side of his personality for the first time or that he was possessed by an alien spirit?

4. The Better Diagnosis. In medicine a correct diagnosis is essential to healing. If a physician misdiagnoses, the patient is much less likely to heal under him than under a different physician who correctly diagnoses. Conversely, it is likely that a physician's diagnosis leading to successful treatment is sounder than a second physician's diagnosis leading to unsuccessful or less successful treatment. All of this is self-evident.

If a patient has symptoms that suggest schizophrenia or psychosis to a typical Western-trained psychotherapist, but suggest possession to a healer or exorcist, equally successful treatment is not likely to come from both. We would expect that the reason the more successful approach worked was that it correctly diagnosed the problem.

Which approach succeeds, or at least succeeds more often, the conventional psychiatric approach which rules out any possibility of spirit oppression from the outset, or the spiritual approach which not only makes room for it but suspects it when the appropriate symptoms are present?

First the psychiatric. Generalizing about the effectiveness of contemporary psychopharmacological treatment for severe mental illness is risky, but there are studies which help. In his book *The Undiscovered Mind* the well regarded science writer, John Horgan, refers to several of these. He concludes:

> . . . chlorpromazine and related medications for schizophrenia have often been described as virtual cures. But according to a leading psychiatric textbook, "a reasonable estimate is that 20 to 30 percent" of schizophrenics taking medication "are able to lead relatively normal lives. Approximately 20 to 30 percent of patients continue to experience moderate symptoms, and 40 to 60 percent remain significantly impaired for life." Moreover, chlorpromazine and other anti-psychotic drugs often cause effects that resemble the symptoms of Parkinson's disease. Patients' movements and facial expressions become stiff and rigid; they display uncontrollable, repetitive twitching and tremors. It was, in part, these side effects that led psychiatrists to call anti-psychotic medications neuroleptics, which literally means "brain-seizers."

But psychiatrists do not rely solely on drugs to manipulate the brain back into sanity. After falling out of favor for a generation, electroconvulsive therapy (ECT, or "shock therapy") has returned to favor because of "the growing recognition of drug limitations." No one in the psychiatric community can say for certain why ECT works, but there is no question that it does. As Dr. Harold Sackheim, a psychologist at Columbia University, says, "Not only is the probability of getting well higher than with any other treatment, but the likelihood of getting residual symptoms is less." ECT is a much more exact science today than it was back in the 20's when Carl Wickland was zapping patients to rid them of possessing spirits (see above), but the treatment is essentially the same.

Now for the spiritual. Do healers, exorcists, shamans, and deliverance ministers fare any better than psychiatrists? I wish I could tell you the Chinese farmer who was freed from two demons and fully recovered his normal personality *stayed cured* but Goullart does not tell us. What about the Indian cases? Stanley, a trained social scientist, gives us a little more to go on:

All healing centers claim a high percentage of cure for victims [of possession] who come regularly to *arati* sessions. Most of the cures are said to require only a few weeks; some, as long as a year. Although I was not able to test these claims in any rigorous way, my conversations with spirit victims and friends and relatives of victims, as well as with people who had been cured, confirmed the claims without exception. Nearly all who come regularly are, after a certain period of time, fully restored to feeling their former selves. Some few do come to sessions regularly for years without complete recovery, but even in these "incurable" cases the relatives and friends of the victim report that the sessions help the individual a great deal—especially that they feel much better immediately after an *arati* session.

I see no reason to doubt the truth of Stanley's report. He is careful not to exaggerate—he acknowledges there are incurable cases—and he has taken care to interview many people in a variety of conditions. And he admits that the possessing spirits have a tendency to return until they are convinced it would be more comfortable for them to re-tire permanently. Moreover, his findings are supported by witnesses of possession-type phenomena in other parts of India.

Back in the United States, psychiatrist Peck, participant in two exor-cisms, holds that exorcism is an effective cure—the only effective cure—in certain situations: "Difficult and dangerous though they were, the exor-cisms I witnessed were successful. I cannot imagine how otherwise the two patients could have been healed. They are both alive and very well today. I have every reason to believe that had they not had their exorcisms they would each be dead by now." And deliverance minister MacNutt adds:

I once prayed for a young woman who had been confined in a mental hospital for twelve years, suffering from schizophrenia. After two hours of prayer for healing and deliverance, the glazed look in her eyes left and she was able to converse in a normal way. Several weeks later the doctors recognized a dramatic change in her behavior and released her from the hospital. I could cite many more examples from a steady stream of supplicants ... unable to find help from psychotherapy or from those who are ministers of religion who had not learned to deal with the demonic.

"Our madhouses," writes Huston Smith, "may contain souls that are ravaged by principalities and powers on the psychic plane; in a word, possessed." MacNutt agrees.

I haven't discovered any statistics showing the relative success and failure of exorcists and deliverance ministers, but my impression, from a study of much anecdotal evidence, is that there are more successes than failures when the required expertise is present. Most important, these successes, when they occur, are usually total, as they were in Peck's two exorcisms, in Martin's five case studies, and in most of Stanley's samples. As a result, it is impossible to avoid arriving at the surprising conclusion, at least for the moment, that evil spirits are real and that they sometimes obsess or possess the living. For if they were not real, then why would an exorcism work? One might just as well bring about a cure for stomach cancer by taking out the appendix. Isn't it reasonable to conclude that exorcism works so dramatically, completely, and permanently in cases where conventional psychiatry fails because the exorcist has correctly diagnosed the ailment and the psychiatrist has not?

There are arguments, some stronger and some weaker, against this conclusion. Here is the one I regard as the strongest:

It has to be acknowledged that drugs and ECT do have an impact on the brain and on the inner life of almost all mentally ill people. As Paul Churchland puts it, "For better or worse, the insane asylums of the 1940's and 50's are now mostly emptied, thanks to first-generation psychopharmaceuticals." Furthermore, recent advances in drug therapy and ECT have ameliorated the situation even more. We are far from having discovered anything close to a cure for schizophrenia or psychosis, or even depression, but, as Churchland says, "we can still do measurable good." And since we can, then it makes sense to conclude that mental illness is an illness of the brain, not a result of spirit-affliction. For it is a lot easier to see why drugs have an impact on a sick brain than on a possessing spirit. Indeed, it is ludicrous, Churchland and other materialists conclude, to think that drugs or ECT are effective because they chase away demons.

This argument requires two responses. First, it must be granted that, however imperfectly, drugs and ECT often do help the mentally ill. But what does this prove? No responsible exorcist or deliverance minister claims that *all* mental illness is caused by the presence of evil spirits. MacNutt, for example, reports that his wife, Judith, when counselling clients as a licensed psychotherapist, "ended up praying with [only] about a third of them to be freed from the influence of evil spirits." This suggests that in the other two-thirds, even a therapist as sensitive to the presence of oppressing spirits as his wife, diagnosed them in only a minority of cases. American clergy commonly distinguish between afflictions that are "purely emotional" and those that are "spiritual." This distinction prevails throughout the deliverance ministry.

Second, it is not at all ludicrous to consider the possibility that drugs and ECT might inhibit spirit oppression or possession. Is it really so preposterous that a spirit utilizing in some mysterious way a person's body, more particularly the brain, should be disturbed or even uprooted when that body with its brain is subjected to a shock as violent as ECT? As I pointed out above, psychiatrists do not know why ECT works. Dr. Sackheim, the psychiatrist working at Columbia, says: "We're triggering a seizure in order to get the brain to stop a seizure.... God knows if it's true." Moreover, is it all that farfetched to consider the further possibility that powerful neuroleptic medications might discourage an obsessing spirit from oppressing its victim, and, like shock therapy, creates a hostile environment in the brain for oppressing spirits? After all, cures of many diseases are administered both topically and internally. Might ECT be the topical approach to expelling an oppressive spirit from the victim's brain, and medication the internal? Not to consider such a possibility, however heterodox, is unscientific.

So what should we conclude? Dr. Peck wrote in 1983 that "possession and exorcism have never been scientifically studied, to my knowledge, in America or Europe." He acknowledges that Western anthropologists have long studied possession phenomena in the Developing World, but India is not America.

I await the day that teams of experienced exorcists, with seven-or-eight-figure grants, will be allowed to treat "hopeless" schizophrenics or psychotics locked away in mental institutions — given up on, in other words — to see if depossession rituals work where drugs failed? We have glimpses of such success. I mentioned above the apparent cure by MacNutt of a schizophrenic who had been in a mental institution for twelve years. And Peck was not the only psychotherapist working in America to treat mental illness as possession. Colin Wilson mentions two who occasionally treated their patients *as if* they were possessed. One of them, Dr. Ralph Allison, a specialist on MPD working in California, occasionally ran into personalities that did not act at all like split-off alters. Of one of these Allison wrote, "Despite all my efforts, I was unable to find a more plausible explanation for his existence than the spirit theory."

But these are only glimpses. We are left with a great deal of tantalizing evidence pointing to spirit oppression or outright possession. We do not have, however, the indubitable evidence (the "slam dunk") we need to overturn the claim of Western medicine that infesting spirits are not the cause — ever — of mental illness.

What would constitute such evidence? Replicability, says science. And I agree. But what would it take to satisfy the demand for replicability? Would the horrific phenomena reported by Goullart — including the weighed-down rock-like body that bends iron bedsteads or the horribly inflated body resembling a balloon—be disqualified from consideration because they could not be replicated on demand in a lab? Or because they turned up in only one out of twenty exorcisms? How many deliverance ministers and healers would have to share their stories in the serious journals and magazines before scientists took note? How many exorcisms like the Chinese case would it take to convince the entrenched skeptics of CSI (Committee for Skeptical Inquiry) that there was no fraud or credulity or misunderstanding, but honest and careful reporting of the facts? What about levitation, a feature of certain advanced cases of possession reported in many cultures in every age down to the present? If occasional cases of levitation by apparently possessed persons were witnessed and videotaped by reputable individuals (and they have been), would the professional debunkers be mollified?

I don't think so. Most materialists deny the existence of even extrasensory perception (ESP). I once had a friend, a psychiatrist, who woke up one night at ten minutes to two and told his wife that his brother had just died. Sure enough, the call came a few hours later that his brother, who had not been sick, had indeed died — sometime around two in the morning. For many months my friend read everything he could find on ESP. But when I talked to him three years after his brother's death, he dismissed the whole affair as an "anomaly," a "coincidence."

Why did this bright man respond in such a way? I think I know. In all that he read, he could find no explanation of how ESP *worked*. The brute fact of his sudden "knowing" about his brother's death was compatible with no scientific (i.e., physicalist) theory he could discover. So he concluded he must have misunderstood what happened. The "knowing" was really nothing more than an illusion.

I believe that this sort of unyielding skepticism will always oppose those who find much evidence for a dualist interpretation of reality. Dualism, beginning with our own immediate experience (*our* bodies), has an enormous amount of evidence in its favor. But, as we will see in chapter 10, it fails to provide an explanation of how immaterial and material substances *interact*; that interaction is almost as mysterious today as it was when Plato defended it. And many people reject it for that reason — along with all those queer experiences, such as spirit oppression, that depend on it.

In spite of the mysteriousness of our subject, I believe that the evidence reviewed here provides extremely good reason to think that Jesus' interpretation of mental illness 2000 years ago is at least sometimes on the mark. If it is, the implications for us would be significant. Most importantly, if an *alien* spiritual being could interact with a living brain, that would suggest all the more strongly that an *inborn* spiritual being — what we call a soul — could interact with it. If so, materialism would have to be discarded, and some form of dualism would replace it. In addition, life after death would become plausible once again. And the human will, no longer a side effect of brain states, could again fly free. Even God might seem more comely after such a metaphysical facelift. If spirits, earthbound or demonic, came to be regarded by intelligent men and women as real, Spirit would again take its place at the controls.

What should psychiatry's response be? Are psychiatrists in this country quietly wondering if there is something to possession? If so, there is no evidence of it that I can find in professional literature. To take but one of many examples, in a psychiatry journal article titled "The Delusion of Possession in Chronically Psychotic Patients," there were frequent references to "delusional possession" and "the delusion of possession" in the 25 of 61 psychotic outpatients who believed themselves possessed. It never occurred to the authors that some of those patients might *really* be possessed. And a few years ago in *Newsweek*, the lead article, "The Schizophrenic Mind," never mentioned possession. Even though the author described schizophrenia as "one of the most . . . mysterious of mental illnesses" and went on to say that the "cause is largely unknown," she, and all the doctors whom she quoted, assumed without question that the illness was caused exclusively by a disordered brain. "In paranoid schizophrenia," she continued, "the patient becomes convinced of beliefs at odds with reality, hears voices that aren't there or sees images that exist nowhere but in his mind." Since she was supported by every psychiatrist she interviewed, she felt it unnecessary to question this claim — indeed it may never have occurred to her to question it. But what is the evidence, after all, that the voices heard by the schizophrenic or the images he sees "exist nowhere but in his mind"? This is an assumption, not a fact. It may well be that the voices belong to realities that we cannot see. Does our inability to see them make them unreal? To a certain kind of materialist, yes. But what about the rest of us? More to the point, does the evidence surveyed here point conclusively to materialism? If anything, taken all together it points with some force in the opposite direction.

There is a telling moment in English author Susan Howatch's novel *Glittering Images* where two of her characters are discussing exorcism. The time is the 1930s:

> "Do they still perform exorcisms in the Church of England?"
>
> "Nowadays it's generally regarded as a somewhat unsavoury superstition."
>
> "How odd! Is it wise for the Church to abandon exorcism to laymen?"
>
> "What laymen?"
>
> "They're called psycho-analysts," she said dryly. "Maybe you've heard of them? They have this cute little god called Freud and a very well-paid priesthood and the faithful go weekly to worship on couches."

This character is not speaking tongue-in-cheek. She is saying that materialists who arrogantly dismiss possessing spirits as the ultimate cause of some mental illness are unscientific.

Over a 22-month period beginning in March 2012, a family in Gary, Indiana, was the focus of events so horrifying that everyone connected with the case, from the city's police chief to the medical personnel of a hospital, could think of no other explanation but possession to account for them. According to the *Indianapolis Star*, Rosa Campbell, the grandmother of three children living in a run-down rented house with their mother, watched as her 12-year-old granddaughter floated unconscious over her bed. Thus began a series of events, including much banging and other poltergeist phenomena, believed to be caused by demonic spirits. In an official report of over a hundred pages, Gary police tell of photographing with their iphones ghosts apparently living in the basement. These events are far too numerous to cover here, but one in particular should give every skeptic special cause for concern.

In April the two other children, boys aged 9 and 7, were taken to a doctor's office for analysis. Dr. Geoffrey Onyeukwu told the *Star* that he was greeted with curses from the children "in a demonic voice" unlike anything he'd seen in twenty years of practice. When the boys passed out, he couldn't make them come to. The police were called in, and the boys were taken to a hospital. *The New York Daily News*, collaborating with *The Star*, took up the story:

> "When both children woke up in a hospital, the youngest began screaming and violently thrashing about. It took five men to hold the 7-year-old boy down," Campbell (the boys' grandmother) told *The Star*.

> DCS (Department of Child Services) family case manager, Valerie Washington, was then called in to evaluate the children. When she met them, the youngest, she reported, started to growl and flash his teeth at her. His eyes then rolled back into his head. Then the 7-year-old lunged for his older brother and put his hands around his throat while saying in a voice that wasn't his own: "It's time to die. I will kill you," according to Washington's report. Once released from his brother's grasp, the 9-year-old allegedly started head-butting his grandmother. Campbell [the grandmother] took his hand and started to pray when the boy walked backward up a wall and onto the ceiling. Once there he flipped and landed perfectly on his feet.

> Washington's DCS report is corroborated by Willie Lee Walker, a registered nurse, who was in the room with them. "He walked up the wall, flipped over her [the grandmother] and stood there," Walker told *The Star*. "There's no way he could've done that."

> Washington, in her report to police, described the boy as "gliding."

In the meantime several exorcisms were performed on the mother, Latoy Ammans, by Rev. Mike Maginot, a Catholic priest. In June, Ammons and Campbell moved back to Indianapolis, and by November the children were again living with their mother. The DCS met with the family and in their assessment found "no demonic presences or spirits in the home."

The *Newsweek* article cited above made it appear to millions of readers that the cause of all mental illness is faulty brain chemistry—no discussion needed! I hope I have shown here that this unexamined assumption is unwarranted.

I suggest that psychiatrists do the following:

1. Challenge the above assumption with philosophical rigor. Especially consider the possibility that a person might be a mix of two different kinds of reality working in harmony when the person is mentally healthy and in disharmony when not. The invisible part of the mix should not be assumed to be unreal or a mere epiphenomenon of brain states just because it is invisible. That reasoning would lead to the assumption that electricity, since invisible, is either unreal or a mere epiphenomenon of the visible light bulb! Who can say that the spiritual component of the person is not like electricity? Surely it is at least possible that the visible brain is the invisible soul's instrument and that the soul empowers the instrument just as electricity powers up the light bulb.

2. Study the responsible literature investigating paranormal phenomena. As we've already seen, over the last fifty years university professors and medical doctors have produced hundreds of books dealing with deathbed visions, the near-death experience, apparitions, poltergeists, mediumship, reincarnation, and possession; and several scientific journals investigate these phenomena at great length. Obviously there is much here to be skeptical about, and indeed there are frauds aplenty making a buck off the gullible simpletons who drink up everything about these perennially fascinating subjects as if it were Coca Cola. But it is a great mistake to assume that every book on the paranormal is untrustworthy. Some of the most significant pioneering studies of the human mind have been written in recent years by university professors with strong academic credentials. Ian Stevenson, working with little children who have memories of a previous life, and Kenneth Ring, who, as we saw earlier, demonstrated that blind people who have an NDE sometimes see for the first time in their lives, come to mind. The conclusions of these two, as well as many other pioneers of consciousness in our quantum age, are the fruit of extremely careful research and should be carefully studied by psychiatrists interested in mapping the human mind. Such study would wean many students from their too-hasty materialist assumptions. They might stay with their materialism, but it would be only after a struggle. Many other students, I predict, would convert to some kind of spirit-body dualism. Materialism would begin to feel to them like the old epicenter theory used in the sixteenth century to bolster the dying geocentric theory of the universe before the Copernican Revolution took hold. For them, materialism would simply fail to account for too many facts.

3. Conduct research to determine whether the tools and techniques of the exorcist and deliverance minister work better than the drugs

and therapies of the psychiatrist. Allow a few battle-tested exorcists and deliverance ministers into mental institutions to work with victims that psychiatry cannot help. If initial results are encouraging, promulgate the findings far and wide. Then write grants for the tens of millions of dollars needed to further test the spiritual techniques that appear to be working. Many trials will be needed and the most sophisticated experiments devised. I predict that by the end of this century the research will have been done and the results will be startling. But why wait for another fifty years? All it takes is for one brave doctor to put his reputation on the line in the interest of truth, and compassion, and get started.

Perhaps fifty years from now *Newsweek* will do another lead article on the schizophrenic mind. And instead of saying that the paranoid schizophrenic "becomes convinced of beliefs at odds with reality, hears voices that aren't there, or sees images that exist nowhere but in his mind," the author will report that "*in some cases* it is almost certain that a hostile or mischievous spiritual being causes its victim to hear voices and see images that emanate not from the mind of the victim but from the mind of the spirit." If that turns out to be the case, then psychiatry will have to turn itself on its head, redesign the curriculum of its medical schools, and get about the business of healing *all types* of mental illness—those that originate in the chemistry of the brain, those that originate in the soul that constantly interacts with and may negatively alter the chemistry of the brain, and those that originate in a meddlesome or hostile spiritual presence targeting, either with or without its victim's permission, the soul or brain of its victim.

Levitation, walking upside down, and other appalling phenomena we've looked at in this chapter are part of our world. To deny them is to pretend, to engage in self-deception. We know that human beings in physical bodies aren't capable of such feats left to themselves. They get help from another form of being, one that most of us can't see, but who seem very much like us at our worst. They have gone before us into the land of death, but they can penetrate our world and do it harm. The worst of them can terrorize it. Like it or not, demonic spirits, along with their less spectacular and far more numerous brethren, whom we refer to as earthbound spirits, form part of the case for human survival. Still another stick, though one we might wish away, has been added to the ensemble.

7.

REINCARNATION CASES

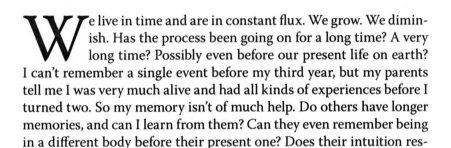

We live in time and are in constant flux. We grow. We diminish. Has the process been going on for a long time? A very long time? Possibly even before our present life on earth? I can't remember a single event before my third year, but my parents tell me I was very much alive and had all kinds of experiences before I turned two. So my memory isn't of much help. Do others have longer memories, and can I learn from them? Can they even remember being in a different body before their present one? Does their intuition resonate with John L. Stoddard's poem "Reincarnation"?

> I know not how, I know not where,
> But from my own heart's mystic lore
> I feel that I have breathed this air,
> And walked this earth before;
>
> And that in this, its latest form
> My old-time spirit once more strives,
> As it has fought through many a storm
> In past, forgotten lives.

The thought of living in a previous body is off-putting to many of us. First, most Jews, Christians, and Muslims explicitly reject reincarnation.

Second, the notion is counter-intuitive; it doesn't "feel right." We're used to getting older, but if reincarnation is true, then we got younger when we took on a newborn baby's flesh a few decades ago. And we might get younger again! Third, we identify ourselves so much with our present body that the thought of being in another body—of being ourselves in another body—is, again, counter-intuitive; it doesn't "feel right." Persons of skeptical disposition are automatically suspicious of it. They want evidence. Is there evidence for reincarnation? Strong evidence? Have we lived several lives on earth? Have we experienced not just one afterlife, but several? Is immortality a roller-coaster ride, with as many ups as downs?

Let me say right up front that I'm not especially pleased at the thought of living several or even many lives on this or any other material planet. I'd prefer to keep on going after death and never look back. But science has taught me that what I'd prefer is not what counts. What counts is the evidence. Anyone who has read Ian Stevenson's work with an open, scientific spirit is likely to come away wondering, if not convinced.

Who is Ian Stevenson? Is he an authority we can trust? Before he retired, he headed the Department of Psychiatry at the University of Virginia. He died in 2007, well into his eighties, doing research right up to the end. He has impeccable academic credentials — hundreds of scholarly articles and more than a dozen books. Today there are quite a few web sites dedicated to exploring his research. He used to do conventional psychiatry, but beginning in 1960 he got into paranormal research when he stumbled across his first reincarnation case in Burma. It changed his life. One of his colleagues said something like, "Either he is making a colossal mistake, or he is the Galileo of the 20th century." For fifty years critics have tried to poke holes in his research. Their criticisms are important, for they keep us from drawing conclusions prematurely. But the edifice so painstakingly built by Stevenson still stands, even though it's far from earthquake-proof. We'll see why below.

You might guess that Stevenson works with subjects who get regressed under hypnosis and start talking about past lives, or who go to a psychic and get a past-life reading. This is not so. Stevenson, in fact, dismisses almost all of this testimony as either fraudulent or self-deceived. He is well aware that con artists often pose as psychics. And he knows that hypnotized subjects are eager to please their hypnotist and supply the details of a "past life" asked for and usually paid for. Though not intentionally trying to deceive the hypnotist, there is the constant danger that their imaginations will run wild and create a scenario on the spot, just as they do in dreams. Stevenson will have none of this.

Almost all of Stevenson's subjects are very young children who remember what feels to them like a past life. Their memories of this life are as vivid, life-like, and – most startlingly – accurate as any child's ordinary memories. In particular they remember their past death.

Stevenson investigated over 2,500 cases of the reincarnation type before he died. Some are stronger than others. About half of them are solved; that is, the person remembered has been matched to the child doing the remembering. Let's consider an ideally developed case.

A child of two, three, or four—let's place her in India and call her Devi—begins talking about a former life in a different village. Devi gives her former name, Sita, and the name of the village. She also names and describes her mother, a favorite sister, and an influential teacher from that life. She tells how she misses life in that village and especially her two children, who were little more than toddlers when she died after being bitten on the toe by a snake. She tells her parents she is homesick and wishes to visit her former home, which is never talked about and has never been visited by anyone in her family.

One day she runs up to an apparent stranger outside her home and, speaking with great joy, calls him "Teacher." The man is startled, and Devi's mother runs up to apologize. But the little girl insists she is Sita and knows him and that he was her teacher back in the other village. By now Devi's parents, both Hindu, begin to wonder if Devi might really be a reincarnation of someone named Sita who lives in a distant village. Her parents begin to talk about their case, and someone brings it to the attention of one of Stevenson's associates living in India. The associate does some preliminary work, ascertains the case is genuine, and identifies a family in the alleged former village matching Devi's description. He even hears about the young mother who died by snakebite some six years earlier. Stevenson, who travels regularly to South Asia to investigate new cases and follow up on old ones, is notified, and he makes plans to visit Devi in a few months. But he does not inform the families – either Devi's or Sita's — of his plans.

When he arrives in the district, his associate takes him to see Devi. He asks the child to talk about her past life, and he writes down everything she says. She describes her home, a small temple across the street dedicated to Rama, a vegetable vendor who had a parrot that could recite one line from the Vedas, and many other particulars. He gets permission from Devi's parents to take her – she is just shy of her fourth birthday – to the alleged former village. He stays overnight in Devi's home, and the next day they set out in an automobile, the first Devi has ever ridden in. It takes two hours to cover the 34 km distance over rutted lanes, and on the way he jots down more of Devi's memories. She shows tremendous excitement.

When they get to the village, the party gets out of the car, and Stevenson asks Devi to lead them to her former home. The child does not hesitate, and they wind their way through narrow lanes, with a curious crowd beginning to gather. "Here is my home," she exclaims, "but it used to be white." Stevenson's associate points out that this is not the house he visited her former family in, but Stevenson notes the temple directly across the street. The residents of the house are unknown to Devi and tell Stevenson's associate they've been renting the house for five years. Then they agree to lead the party to the landlord's home.

When they arrive there, Devi recognizes an uncle and runs up to him, telling him she is Sita. He is amazed but remembers the earlier visit from Stevenson's associate. He tells the party to wait and sets out at a run. He returns with a dozen people around him, and Sita squeals in delight. First she runs to her mother, then turns to her two children, now much bigger than she is, and begins to talk to them using terms of endearment that her husband, also present with his new wife, recognizes. It's clear she knows most of the people her uncle brought along, and most become convinced that Devi is indeed Sita. They also verify that her former home was white, that she died of snakebite, and that the vendor with the parrot still makes his rounds. Someone produces a family photograph, and she points to and names most of the faces. She asks about her favorite sister, but she has married and moved to a different town. When it's time to go, Devi/Sita begs to stay with her old family, but she's carried away waving and shrieking.

In the following months she asks repeatedly to be taken for another visit. But once she starts school, the old memories begin to fade, and so does her interest in a visit. Eventually she learns to regard her present mother as her "true mother." Stevenson visits Devi seven years later and finds her a normally developing girl with only the vaguest memories of her former life.

What do we do with a case like this? If it were unique, it would certainly arouse curiosity, but it would not convince. What's so convincing about Stevenson's research (and his successor Jim Tucker's) is the sheer number of cases like the above. Described in bland academic prose, published by the University Press of Virginia for consumption by scholars, they are no easy target for debunkers. Dr. Albert Stunkard, a professor of psychiatry at the University of Pennsylvania Medical School, said of him: "I know there are a lot of people who disagree with him, but most of their criticism is done without reviewing his work. He's an incredible methodologist, hard to fault. He's very convincing, but I'm not convinced. Which is not to say that his research isn't valid."

And that might be your response too. But if it is, I suspect that, like Dr. Stunkard, Stevenson's findings are just too hard to believe; they have crossed your "boggle threshold." But what are the alternatives? How do you explain what happened to Devi if reincarnation is not true?

There are two somewhat plausible alternatives. The first was put forth by John Hick, the eminent philosopher of religion who once disbelieved in reincarnation on philosophical grounds, but a few years before his death changed his mind and adopted reincarnation as the more likely explanation of the facts Stevenson kept turning up.

I call it the "mental corpse" theory, and it goes like this. We all know that our living body turns into a lifeless corpse at death. What about our living mind? What happens to it? Instead of being wiped out without a trace, maybe it leaves behind a corpse of its own, a mental corpse. Since the mind is invisible, its corpse would also be invisible, so we cannot see it; we cannot see where it is or where it is not. We can think of it as floating freely somewhere in the atmosphere. Now a mental corpse is full of information, of memories belonging to the person whose living mind it used to be. It's like an invisible hard drive with an enormous amount of information on it, but the information is useless without a living mind to "read" it. And that is what the young, unformed, impressionable mind of Devi does when it makes contact with Sita's mental corpse. And that's how Devi knows so much about Sita's life and even comes to regard Sita's life as her own. This theory, if true, would explain all the facts of the case, but without assuming reincarnation.

The main problem with the mental corpse theory is that there is no evidence of such a thing. No one has interviewed or photographed or knowingly bumped up against one. Yet that doesn't mean it doesn't exist. Maybe science will establish its existence in the future.

For me it boils down to what is more bizarre: mental corpses or reincarnation? Keep in mind that reincarnation has mysteries of its own. One of them is how a living, conscious being with a rich history could make contact with a fetus and embed all this history into a newly hatched physical organism's brain.

The second alternative to reincarnation is possession. This theory says that Devi can remember much of Sita's life because Sita is an earthbound spirit who has taken possession of, or is sharing, Devi's little body and young impressionable mind. As a result, little Devi not only knows her own parents and siblings and immediate environment, but has memories of Sita's as well.

Stevenson gives a lot of attention to this hypothesis in cases like De-vi-Sita; he regards it as the greatest challenge to reincarnation. He admits his arguments are less than compelling to everyone, but he does feel that the reincarnation hypothesis is much more plausible. In cases of possession, labeled "spirit possession syndrome" by professionals who work in this area, the possessing spirit (or what seems to be a possessing spirit) usually interferes with the healthy development of its victim: the result is mental and sometimes physical illness. But the very young children who, according to this theory, are overshadowed by an alien mind, don't show such symptoms. They do not need to be released (or exorcised, to use an old-fashion term) from an attached spirit in order to recover their health. Furthermore, we would expect a radical and almost immediate alteration in the victim's personality once the alien spirit departed, but in fact we see a gradual, barely noticeable change, typically begun when the child starts school. Stevenson asks a further question: "Why should all possessing personalities quit their victims when the children are at about the same age?" For these and several other reasons Stevenson sees reincarnation as a far better hypothesis. In any case, both reincarnation and possession require survival of bodily death.

There are other cases that point to reincarnation with greater force. Stevenson's *Reincarnation and Biology*, a massive two-volume work of over 2300 pages, is a study of 200 children with distinctive bodily features. All of them remember being people who received wounds, usually fatal, corresponding to birthmarks or birth defects on their new bodies. (They aren't usually aware of these marks or defects until later, but their parents usually note them from the time of birth.) His book contains many photographs of these blemishes; in the best cases he's discovered medical records, sometimes even sketches, of the wounds on the victim's body. To make this clearer, let's suppose that Devi, in addition to everything else we know about her, has a birthmark on her foot that corresponds to the bite of the snake that took Sita's life — or to the incisions her uncle made with his knife to suck out the venom. Stevenson actually has several snakebite cases just like this. More dramatically, let's suppose that Sita, instead of being killed by snake-bite, was accidentally shot in the head, and that Devi has twin birth-marks, one corresponding to the entry point of the bullet that killed Sita, the other to the exit point. Stevenson has 18 cases like this. He figures the odds of all these cases being explained by coincidence at one in about 25,000.

Now Stevenson feels he's on much firmer ground. Clearly no possessing spirit produced the scar, for the child was born with the scar.

But how does a spirit, whoever it might be, produce a scar on its prenatal body? What does Stevenson say about this? One thing modern medicine has taught us in the last twenty years is that mental states profoundly affect our bodies. We can make ourselves sick by constantly feeling anger or stress, and we can help our bodies heal by positive thinking. No doctor knows better than an oncologist that the cancer patient's attitude is often a crucial factor in her response to treatment. And many psychologists are willing to grant that happiness and sadness sometimes affect brain chemistry rather than the other way round. Stevenson's explanation of the birthmarks on his children is that a sustained mental image, usually connected to the traumatic death of the previous personality, has influenced the development of the embryo. This interpretation is consistent with the reincarnation hypothesis, not possession. For this reason Stevenson considers cases involving birthmarks and birth defects as the strongest indicators of reincarnation. The reincarnation hypothesis, for Stevenson, is now on very solid ground.

There are other factors that point to reincarnation. A few weeks ago I was talking to a Christian woman whose husband is an identical (or one-egg) twin, but whose personality from the beginning of life was nothing like his brother's; he has always been rational and cool-head-ed (he's a retired judge), his brother aggressive and hot-tempered. Yet their parents raised them the same way; there was no difference in their early environment. She was startled when I told her that such cases provide a strong argument for reincarnation. "They have identical genetic material," I said. "How could they be so different?" Stevenson points out that these contrasting personality traits are very probably "derived from previous lives."

But previous lives explain more than personality; they can account for phobias, unusual aptitudes, and what Stevenson calls "gender-identity confusion." Regarding phobias, I live next door to a woman who gives individualized swimming lessons to children in her backyard pool. Every summer there is at least one "screamer"—a child who has no identifiable reason to fear water but who shrieks to high heaven when placed in the warm and inviting water of Kim's lovely pool. Such children don't shriek only once, but every time they come over, usually once a week. In most cases she eventually frees them of their phobia. On talking to her I learned she had no explanation for the behavior she's been observing for 25 years. Stevenson discovered that "among forty-seven cases in which the previous personality drowned, a phobia of being immersed in water occurred in thirty (64 percent)." Did I dare mention reincarnation to Kim? I couldn't resist, and she has thought me odd ever since. I should point out that the screamers, as far as I know, have no imaged memory of such a drowning. According to Stevenson that is usual.

Other kids do have memories of their previous life, and these sometimes give rise to special aptitudes or addictive habits that cannot be accounted for by their upbringing. "I have known two children," Stevenson says, "who remembered the lives of alcoholics and in their play gave amusing demonstrations of how a drunken person staggers around and collapses." "Many subjects," he adds, "have expressed in their play the vocation of the previous personality."

Of special interest is what Stevenson refers to as "gender-identity confusion." Reincarnation is arguably the best explanation for cases in which a three-year-old acts the part of a child of the opposite sex. Stevenson explains:

> The children who say they remember previous lives as a member of the opposite sex nearly always show, when young, traits that are characteristic of the claimed former sex. They may reject, or act as if they rejected, the anatomical sex of their bodies. A girl, for example, may assert that she is a boy and insist on dressing in boys' clothes, playing boys' games, and being addressed as a boy would be.

He goes on to say that the majority gradually learn to accept their anatomical sex and "become normal in all respects," but that a few "have remained fixed in the gender role of the sex of the previous life and usually are correspondingly unhappy."

Stevenson cites several psychologists who claim that such behavior in little boys usually leads to homosexuality later in life. "I suggest," writes Stevenson, "that a previous life as a person of the opposite sex may initiate in a child a sexual orientation toward the opposite sex without, however, permanently fixing it." This is far from a complete-ly satisfactory explanation of homosexuality, but given the disarray of opinion about its ultimate etiology—is it genetic or is it generated by what parents do to the child in the first few years? It is worth consid-ering. It makes sense, in my view better sense than the alternatives.

Another mystery is the rejection by some children of their parents in favor of previous ones. In the case we looked at earlier, Devi never goes so far as to say to her mother, "You are not my real mother; my real mother lives in . . ." But many other children who remember a previous life have said just that. How can this unnatural claim be ac-counted for? It is possible to dislike your mother, but to tell her she's not one's real mother—that is something else. Stevenson thinks he may have the explanation and relates it, interestingly, to infantile autism:

> I suggest that such alienation may derive from unhappy experiences in a previous life, even when the child has no imaged memories of one. This conjecture obviously opposes the view that infantile autism derives exclusively from biological, principally genetic, factors.

Summing up, I have tried to show that, not only does reincarnation seem almost required to explain the accuracy of remembered events in a child's alleged former life, but that other factors, while lacking the clout of this most basic form of evidence, lend further credence to this conclusion.

A discussion of reincarnation wouldn't be complete without ref-erence to what is often termed "age regression"—or regression under hypnosis to memories from a former life. That such a regression guid-ed by a skilled therapist may help clients heal from conflicts, phobias, and traumas is usually acknowledged by psychologists; but "accepting the stories recounted under hypnosis" as valid memories "simply be-cause their airing seems to have aided their patients" is "an unjustified leap." This is the opinion of James G. Matlock, one of the world's fore-most authorities on reincarnation.

Stevenson, as we saw earlier, agrees with Matlock, as does Steven-son's successor Jim Tucker. Stevenson explains:

> Many persons who attach no importance whatever to their dreams—realizing that most of them are merely images of the dreamer's subconscious mind without correspondence to any other reality—nevertheless believe that whatever emerges during hypnosis can

invariably be taken at face value. In fact, the state of a person during hypnosis resembles in many ways—although not in all—that of a person dreaming. The subconscious parts of the mind are released from ordinary inhibitions and they may then present in dramatic form a new "personality." If the subject has been instructed by the hypnotist—explicitly or implicitly—to "go back to another place and time" or given some similar guidance, the new "personality" may appear to be one of another period of history. Such evoked "previous personalities" may be extremely plausible both to the person having the experience and to other persons watching him or her.

Stevenson concludes that "nearly all hypnotically induced 'previous lives' are manifestly bogus."

Many regression therapists seem to be unaware that the "memories" provided by their clients are very probably fabricated. Dr. Brian Weiss is perhaps the most notable. In *Many Lives, Many Mansions*, he tells how he stumbled into regression therapy when one of his clients spontaneously began describing a life in ancient Egypt. In later sessions she mentioned two additional lives from that time, and he asked her if he had been present in any of them. She answered:

> You are my teacher, sitting on a ledge. You teach from books. You are old with gray hair. You're wearing a white dress [toga] with gold trim... Your name is Diogenes. You teach us symbols, triangles. You are very wise, but I don't understand. The year is 1668 B.C.

Stevenson, Tucker, and Matlock all agree that this is a classic example of a client being led by her therapist to construct a personality that exists only in her imagination. The events described are no more reliable than dreams. "They may include some accurate historical details," Stevenson grants, "but these are usually derived from information the subject has acquired normally through reading, radio and television programs, or other sources."

But there are rare exceptions that have evidential value and point with great force to an earlier life. The most compelling case I know of— Jim Tucker brought it to my attention—belonged to a patient named Linda Dilmen (L.D.). She grew up in the Chicago area in the 1940s, later became a school teacher, and was married with two children. Under hypnosis she showed a precise knowledge of hundreds of obscure historical facts from 16th century Spain, where she believed herself to live as a woman named Antonia during the time of the Inquisition. Her therapist, Linda Tarazi, told her story in the *Journal of the American Society for Psychical Research* (1990). For anyone interested in evidence of reincarnation via hypnotic regression, this is the gold standard, the "best of kind." It is possible that the entire story, with all pertinent facts, originated from a discarnate personality with whom L.D. was in telepathic communication, but this possibility strikes both Tarazi and L.D. as farfetched. More likely is the following, which comprises Tarazi's concluding remarks:

> To her (L.D.) it is a definite one-to-one reincarnation, not a blending of ideas from Antonia with her own personality. She has the same traits, talents, and interests as Antonia because she is Antonia reincarnated. Her body contains the soul of Antonia, modified by additional experience. Of course, L.D.'s belief does nothing to validate this theory. Still, it is the only one which, by itself, can account for the personality, feelings, and attitudes of Antonia, as well as for all the obscure historical facts reported, simply and reasonably. Therefore, I tend to concur with L.D.

I cannot begin to suggest to the reader the impressiveness of this case in so few words, especially the painstaking research that Tarazi herself undertook, including trips to Cuenca, Spain, over a three-year period to compare Antonia's claims to recorded facts on 400-year-old records. But evidential accounts like hers are very much the exception.

Before leaving reincarnation, it is worth noting that many people are drawn to belief in it for one of several reasons. Gandhi, a Hindu, seems, unsurprisingly, never to have doubted it. He regarded reincarnation as a great mercy. He asked us to imagine why God declined to give us one long earth life of hundreds or even thousands of years, but chose rather to give us many lives of much shorter duration. He thought he knew the answer. He asked us to consider the mess that most of us make of our lives. Many of us have ruined our reputations, or even our very lives, by foolish choices; and as a result the world looks upon us with contempt. Others nurse hatreds, resentments, and jealousies that squeeze the sweetness out of us. Still others have been scarred by psychological or sexual abuse. Some even have been driven insane by pressures they could not handle. Imagine how miserable most of us would be if forced to live with all this debris for a thousand uninterrupted years.

Most of us need a fresh start. Or at least we know people we love who do. Reincarnation is God's way of providing them. So says Gandhi.

But the most alluring feature of the reincarnation hypothesis for many is the scope it gives for working out justice. The thinking goes like this. We expect people to pay for their crimes, if only by suffering in some fashion the consequences of their deeds. We expect justice in our world, and we expect God to insure it where we fail. It is easy to adapt reincarnation to these expectations, to see it as the means by which justice is served. Hence most reincarnationists build into their system a "law of karma," or law of the deed, in which we are rewarded for the good we do and punished for the evil. A murderer would himself fall victim to violence in a future life; an ungenerous heiress would be reborn into a pauper's home; a bright man who wasted his mind would forfeit his gift next time round. A dedicated musician who lacked the genius to make a dent in the world this time round would be equipped to realize his dream in his next life. A physically unattractive woman who rose above her circumstances and refused to hate a world that was often cold or indifferent to her would enjoy physical beauty in a fresh body. And so forth. Most of us feel comfortable in such a world; most of us could make our peace with a God who governed things so rationally. Thus the belief has religious value.

But is there any evidence that reincarnation actually works this way? If there were, we might find the doctrine not only probably true, but desirable. Let's look at this question in more depth.

If anyone is in a position to answer this intriguing question, it is, again, Ian Stevenson. He can easily compare the lives of hundreds of his subjects – one earth life in the present, another in a not-very-distant past. How might they compare? Does the second life seem to grow justly out of the earlier? Does the law of karma seem to govern their relation?

Stevenson devotes the last section of his most accessible book, *Children Who Remember Previous Lives*, to this question. He sums up his findings:

> In the cases that I have investigated, I have found no evidence of the effects of moral conduct in one life on the external circumstances of another. When I examine the cases that include the feature of a marked difference in socioeconomic status between the families concerned, I can discern no pattern indicating that the vicious have been demoted in this respect and the virtuous promoted.

The prominent reincarnation researcher Jim Matlock comes to a similar conclusion. He finds "no reason to think that the new parents were chosen to punish or reward spirits for their behavior in previous lives." But that's not where it ends. Stevenson continues:

> The children just mentioned, however, did not all remain set in the attitudes of the previous lives, and I have had the pleasure of hearing about, and occasionally observing, the development of different habits in some of them. In these evolutions we see the effect of new environments perhaps; but I think we also see the inner growth of personalities, accomplished only by the self working on itself.

In other words, the socioeconomic, or what he calls the external circumstances of our rebirth don't have much to do with a supposed law of karma working itself out. If this law is at work, it shows itself in other ways. What are these ways?

Stevenson finds that it's common, even normal, for people to reincarnate in the same immediate or extended family they were members of in their previous incarnation. In Myanmar (Burma) and several other regions of the world, stay-at-home cases are the norm. In a few indigenous tribes of northwestern North America ("Eskimos"), it's not uncommon for a person to choose his or her parents in the next life before he or she dies. The rule is that ties of love, affection, and friendship bind. But sometimes animosities or a sense of guilt or indebtedness attract. Attractions, both of love and hate, usually mean that individuals are reborn in the same geographical area they left at death. Even when the individual's two families are not related, they are usually located within 15 miles of each other in non-Western societies. In rare cases an individual is reborn a continent away from where he died. In these cases Stevenson can usually find a logical explanation for such an anomaly, but not always. Either way, it's obvious to him that "physical distance is no impediment" to reincarnation.

It might appear, then, that a law of karma is not in control of the process since family ties seem to trump every other influence. Maybe a young man murders a rival in a fit of jealousy over a woman and is later killed by his victim's brother, or maybe this same young man, choosing a different course, accepts his loss, forgives his vanquisher, and gets on with life, only to die of a disease a little later. Either way, Stevenson finds that it is likely the young man would have the same parents and probably the same newborn body. Where is the law of karma in this? Or consider Bill and Melinda Gates. Lately they have been giving away tens of billions of dollars of their enormous wealth to worthy charities. Suppose they had ignored the moral obligation to share their wealth with the poor or diseased. According to Stevenson, their parents and new bodies next time round would quite possibly be the same either way. But wouldn't we like to see the generous Bill Gates reborn in a wealthy Silicon Valley family, and the stingy Bill Gates reborn in a poor family in a San Jose slum? If this does not happen, isn't the law of karma flouted?

No, says Stevenson, and here's why. Stevenson shows in case after case that personality traits and special skills or aptitudes in the previous life are carried over into the next. Whatever conditions he is reborn into, these traits and skills will be tested. He will have plenty of scope to develop them further or altogether new ones. Whether reborn as a wealthy man or a poor woman, the way he meets life's challenges will determine whether he grows in wisdom and love or just marks time. Isn't it unwise to think the Governor of our world – let's call Him (or Her) God – sees wealth as we do? We see it as something greatly to be desired, but God, if I am right, sees it only as a special kind of challenge for growing our souls, just as God sees poverty as a different kind of challenge. Anyone who is rich or knows someone who is rich is aware that riches are seldom, by themselves, conducive to nobility of character. And that is the only thing, let us hope, that God ultimately cares about. But if the point of our lives is to grow our souls, who is to say how that is best accomplished across several lifetimes? As long as we retain our hard-earned nobility of character from one life to the next—"character karma" let's agree to call it—then justice is served in the highest sense. Stevenson's findings are in line with this complex view of karma, not with a tit-for-tat formulaic view–which he calls "retributive karma"—suggesting that Hitler must come back over and over as a Jew and through countless lives be subjected to every conceivable brutality until his karmic debt is paid.

Stevenson admits that he is on somewhat shaky ground in his speculations about karma and that he "may have said too much." Here is why. The great majority of his subjects died young, and most of these died by violence or by accident. And the average length of time between death and rebirth, covering thousands of cases, is "usually less than three years." In other words, they are a special class of people–not at all like most of us. And their peculiarity, Stevenson suspects, might obscure the way the law of karma works itself out for people like us who live long lives and usually die from a disease. First of all, should we expect, if reincarnation is true, to spend "less than three years" on the Other Side before being reincarnated? And if we spend much more time than three years, are we as likely to remember our past lives? We know from our own experience that the more distant events of our lives are the ones most often forgotten. Now what might we expect to remember of a previous life if we had stayed on the Other Side for seventy or eighty years instead of two or three? Probably nothing at all. If life on the Other Side is an orderly, instructive, "soul-building" kind of place, then many years on earth would normally translate into a longer stay on the Other Side. In other words, Stevenson is aware, and wants us to be aware, that he may be dealing with too narrow a sample of souls – those who usually died young and often by violence — to form a safe idea of how a supposed law of karma applies to most of us. It may well be that a long friendship built up on the Other Side, to take only one example, can result in a person being reborn, not into his previous earthside family, but into the family of his spirit friend. It might also be the case that one's character or talent built up over a long earth life would require, not just the next available family fetus, but a more finely calibrated one in an unrelated family. Furthermore, karmic force might be so exquisitely calibrated that it can guide the single most appropriate sperm—out of three-hundred million or so available in each ejaculation—to the ovum, thus providing the reincarnating soul with precisely the best environment for its further evolution. According to this view, the length of your nose and color of your eyes might be karmically determined. Stevenson finds no evidence of such determination, but he doesn't find any against it either. It's an open question.

I bear a striking resemblance to one of my great grandfathers. I find myself wondering from time to time if I am he. If I am, perhaps one of my grandchildren will someday look at my portrait and wonder if he is me. If reincarnation is true, I have no desire to repeat the grade. But if doing so is the most efficient way to grow my soul further, then I would be foolish to resist.

Voltaire said, "It is not more surprising to be born twice than once; everything in nature is resurrection." Which is more surprising – that after an infinity of time during which we didn't exist we were born for the first time, or that after being born once, several, or many times before, we were born still one more time? When we look at the seasons, with their theme of death and rebirth, can we be surprised if we should be part of that theme? There is a logic to reincarnation that makes sense.

Raynor Johnson, a physicist by training and student of the paranormal by avocation, states the logic somewhat differently:

> If the general conception of evolution be regarded as applicable to the soul as well as to the physical world, it is not either improbable or unreasonable that the soul would adventure forth into the physical world in a newly-built body to acquire further experience of the kind which this world can provide. The fact that the soul has done so once was presumably for adequate and compelling reasons, and whatever these are, it is apparent that more might be gained by a series of such incarnations.

In my earlier book *Heaven and Hell Unveiled* I asked if I found more evidence to think of myself as a young soul with no previous history, or an old soul with a rich past drawn from several incarnations. From all that we've considered in this chapter, it seems very likely that some of us have lived before. Is it logical to take a next step and conclude that since some of us survive death and go on to another life, then all of us must? Or is it just as logical to conclude that, depending on our life choices, some of us might not have to reincarnate—because we learned the necessary lessons that earth provides? If the purpose of life is to evolve into better beings, as spirits speaking through mediums continually tell us, then it would be pointless for all to keep coming back, as if all were destined to experience a common fate. There would be a time to graduate, individual by individual.

This question aside, the evidence for reincarnation surveyed here seems to show with great force that some humans have lived a previous life. If they have, then they have obviously survived their previous death. That being so, it's logical to assume we will too—unless they have a nature unlike ours. But there is no evidence that they do, and every evidence that we all share a common human nature.

One more stick has been added to the ever strengthening bundle.

8.

INSTRUMENTAL TRANSCOMMUNICATION (ITC)

Imagine hearing a voice on a radio or digital recorder that cannot be accounted for by normal means. For example, you have turned your radio dial to a setting unused by any nearby broadcasting station, and all you hear is the steady, uninterrupted rushing or hissing sound of "white noise," or what you might call static. You have patiently listened to that boring noise for as long as a half hour three times a week over a period of two months. You hoped to get a message from someone on the Other Side, someone you love. But you did not call out to anyone specifically, either mentally or physically. Suddenly a somewhat muffled voice cuts through that noise and calls out in hurried, rather weird speech—your name—and then adds, "It's your Granny!" Your grandmother died fourteen years ago, and her memory is dear to you.

This is one example of Instrumental Transcommunication, or ITC. When the means of communication is a voice rather than a picture or text (on a TV or computer monitor, for example), it is often referred to as EVP, short for Electronic Voice Phenomena. All forms of ITC involve communication with intelligences that apparently live beyond our world and are accessed with the aid of an electronic instrument. These intelligences consistently tell us they are deceased human beings. To increase the likelihood of such communication, careful preparation, some of it technical, is usually necessary. We will discuss the technical challenges a little later.

But sometimes an ITC occurs spontaneously, with no preparation, at least on our part. Often the instrument is the telephone. Here is an actual example collected by Callum Cooper, a lecturer on parapsychology at the University of Northampton and author of *Telephone calls from the Dead*:

> My wife's mother has just died, 11 July 1978, from cancer. It was just about a week after she passed away we were getting ready to visit my wife's grandmother in West Virginia. I had gone to the store and my wife was out back in our garden picking vegetables to give away so they wouldn't go to waste while we were gone. She heard the phone ringing, she said it rang several times and she didn't think she would get to it in time but it kept ringing. When she answered it the voice on the other end said: "Jessy [only her mother and brother called her that] this is mommy don't you worry about me now cause I'm all right."

A third form of ITC is visual. In the 1980s, ITC experimenters in Germany and Luxembourg picked up images of deceased friends and pastoral scenes of the afterworld on TV and computer screens. An audio contact had earlier alerted the experimenters when and where the pictures would be found on these instruments, and there they were.

Tens of thousands of ITC researchers, some of them well-meaning amateurs and others credentialed professionals with awards acknowledging their work, are getting occasionally impressive results. But no one has generated more excitement recently than the multilingual Portuguese diplomat Anabela Cardoso. Her 2010 book, *Electronic Voices: Contact with Another Dimension*, is a fascinating autobiography of one woman's quest to make contact with the dead utilizing radios, tape recorders, digital recorders, and microphones. The main key to her eventual success was sheer persistence. What she discovered for herself was that the dead must be wooed. The reason is not that they want to make themselves scarce, but that making contact with us through our clumsy instruments has challenges for them that we cannot appreciate. For them it is, apparently, hard work.

She had read about the successes of earlier ITC experimenters before she began her own quest in 1997. Interestingly, her motivation was practical. A desperately unhappy, suicide-prone woman (Lola) had lost her 18-year-old son in a boating accident and wanted to know if there was any way she could get in touch with him. A few friends knew of Cardoso's interest in afterlife research and put the woman in touch with her. Cardoso decided to make the attempt after Carlos Fernandez, a local electrical technician, showed interest in the experiment.

They proceeded down a well-worn path used by ITC researchers around the globe:

> My method each time I experimented was simply to tune my [two] radios to the wavelengths mid-way between two transmitting stations, so that all I could hear was the hiss of random noise, commonly called 'white noise'. The volume was always set at a comfortable listening level.

Then, sometimes accompanied by Lola or Carlos, she would turn on the tape recorder and ask questions to any spirit that might be listening. For almost three months, on playing back the tape to see if there were any voices, they heard nothing but the sound of their own questions and the hiss. But on January 17, 1998, an anomalous, inexplicable voice answered. From that point on the replies became, in her words, "quite frequent and often of very good acoustic quality." Some of the voices were "as loud and clear as a normal voice speaking to me in the same room." She described them "as a marvel to hear, something that one has to witness personally, to see them happen in front of one's own eyes and to hear them with one's own ears, to fully realize their magical nature." But the best was yet to come.

On March 11, 1998, seated on the floor with her two friends, and radios turned on, Anabela Cardoso asked the unseen communicators if the good-quality replies they were now routinely getting came from an *organized group* dedicated to the mission of communicating with earth. It was a rather daring question, and to her astonishment "a loud masculine voice suddenly erupted from the loudspeaker of the old valve radio, obviously speaking to me.... my surprise was indescribable and I felt a tremendous inner shock." This voice did not rely on a tape to be heard when played back; it exploded, somehow, from the radio itself. Here is a literal, word-for-word translation of what the voice said in Portuguese:

> We are listening to everything. We want to know about the world.

We want to hear your things. Now we are going to count on you, to offer what is just! I was not the one who spoke, but I suppose you have made a question! This is very very difficult! Another world!

This was not the first time that a mysterious voice, apparently from the Other Side, used a radio in this way. The celebrated pioneer of ITC research, Friedrich Jürgenson, had discovered it in the early 1960s when following instructions from taped voices. It became known as the Direct Radio Voices (DRV) method. Cardoso describes it:

... this new channel allows the apparent communicators to interact with the experimenter on Earth by speaking directly through the loudspeaker of a radio. In consequence, anybody present in the room during the experimental session can listen to and even put questions to the communicators who sometimes even exchange views with those present. An astounding conversation can then take place.

Cardoso continues:

I used to ask them all kinds of questions, from philosophical ones on the meaning and purpose of life, to more trivial ones such as the living conditions of my beloved deceased family members and my pets in their new world, and many others on the nature of their world.

I realize that this might seem unbelievable to some readers. "How can we trust her?" they might wonder. Fortunately for us all, one of the world's leading parapsychologists, David Fontana (whom we met in the chapter on poltergeists), observed her on several occasions, and years apart, conversing in Portuguese in her homes in both France and Spain, where she was serving as a senior Portuguese diplomat.

Fontana, a fastidious scientist ever on the lookout for fraud, devised a test to rule it out. He decided to engage the spirits on his own. He asked them to speak to him in English if they could. Specifically, could they repeat after him the words "Hello David" and "How are you?" Seconds later those very words came through the same radio through which the communicators had been speaking to Cardoso. Fontana explains further:

An important feature of this test was that I had said nothing about it beforehand to Dr. Cardoso or indeed to anyone else, and had never suggested that it would be useful to see if the communicators could repeat words offered by me. Thus it would have been impossible for Dr. Cardoso to have made provision in advance to fake these results be pre-recording the replies and, for reasons already outlined, the suggestion that an accomplice might have been involved in any of the work carried out in the studio is untenable.

The most famous paranormal radio communication to date was heard by over a million Europeans tuned into Radio Luxembourg in 1983. Hans Otto König, an electrical-acoustic engineer and leading German ITC researcher, was invited to give a demonstration of direct-voice communication with another world. Radio Luxembourg technicians set up the equipment, and the program's well-known presenter, Rainer Holbe, introduced König. One of the technicians then asked if there was anyone out there with something to say. A voice answered in clear English through the equipment, "Otto König makes wireless with the dead." After a further question the voice said, "We hear your voice." Holbe, with a reputation to protect, said in a shaky voice, "I swear by the life of my children nothing has been manipulated. There are no tricks. It is a voice and we do not know from where it comes." He was so impressed by the communication that he publicly defended König's character, did his own research into ITC, and eventually wrote a book about the experience. The German physicist Professor Ernst Senkowski had observed König on other occasions, sometimes under controlled conditions, when he solicited responses from the voices. Senkowski reported, "The content of the messages and the process of communication leave no doubt about the paranormality of the voices . . . we must conclude that the origin of the voices is in the spirit area in which our departed now reside." Other European researchers, mainly German, left behind thousands of recordings of these voices on tape. A full history of ITC research around the world in the 20th century would fill several library shelves.

One of the most remarkable aspects of the Direct Radio Voices (DRV) is the claim made that they communicate to us through transmitting centers, or "stations." The one we hear most from, and that Cardoso was in constant contact with, named itself in Portuguese *Rio do Tempo—Timestream* in English, *Zeitstrom* in German. Cardoso explains that the richest communications invariably come from stations like Rio do Tempo. The celebrated ITC researcher Konstantin Raudive appears to be the first to discover them. In his famous book

Breakthrough he writes:

> The astonishing conception that "other-worldly" transmitting stations exist emerges quite clearly from many of the voices' statements. Information received indicates that there are various groups of voice-entities who operate their own stations.

Cardoso was for eight years in steady contact with Rio do Tempo until communications broke off in 2007, only to pick up two years later. Today they continue. Over the years she has learned more and more about the voices and their world. First, they tell her emphatically that they are the deceased. And in some ways they are very much like us. For example, they "study, invent, develop and use special devices and technological equipment" to get their messages across, just as we do to reach out to them. Moreover, it is "a lot of work for us," they say. Cardoso confided that "the majority of the voices . . . express themselves with what sound like a tremendous effort." Rio do Tempo tells us that their world "is also a physical world," though vibrating at a frequency that separates ours from theirs. Thus it is legitimate, Cardoso says, "to consider that such things as equipment and stations equally exist in the next physical world that some of us like to call the 'spirit world'."

We saw earlier that Cardoso began serious attempts at communicating with spirits out of compassion for a desperate friend. But her personal quest has always been to learn as much as possible about the world we will all enter at death and that her deceased loved ones enjoy now. Thus she has consistently requested from her invisible friends information about the nature of their world. Fontana summarizes what they have told her:

> The recorded replies [mostly on tape] to this request insist that survival is a natural law for all beings, including plants; that fundamentally all beings are equal; that this world and the next are very similar; that beings in the next world have "bodies"; that suffering in this world is very important for spiritual development; that people in this world should always think of the next world because "Whoever thinks of [the next] world reduces the distances"; that reincarnation is a sporadic event and happens "only when there is no other way"; that Group Souls (groups to which like-minded souls belong) are a reality; that mediumship in the investigator is not necessary in order to receive EVP or DRV communications; and that entities in the next world are

"outside time" and live "on an edge of space" (whatever that means).

But what happens to the beings who live in this environment? According to Cardoso:

> Humans who speak from the next world seem to be profoundly transformed, although not in the sense that the concept of 'beautiful angels floating on clouds' would imply. They are transformed in a thorough, deeply understanding and truly developed way.

Her Rio do Tempo friends tell her that communication by telepathy with each other and with us on earth is a common feature of life in the afterworld. Other abilities that "we would not understand" are hinted at. Much of what they say through our instruments is reminiscent of the worlds described by mediums.

Our deceased friends and loved ones give every evidence of wanting to talk to us, and we of course are more than eager to hear from them. We would like to receive messages as thorough, as nuanced, and as clear as those we get from the best mediums. But progress has not come easy in spite of the fact that great numbers of researchers, from professional parapsychologists with the most sophisticated instruments to ill-equipped dabblers, are working in this area.

From the beginning, as we've seen, anomalous voices emerged from a background of static hiss, or what we now call white noise. Early researchers discovered that this background helped the production of the voices; without that, there was seldom any possibility of contact. The reason for this has never been clear, but right up to the present moment experimenters seeking contact with these voices depend on it. The problem is obvious: all too often the noise drowns out or distorts the voices. ITC professionals are always experimenting with better instruments.

Even when the voices come through clearly, they do not sound like ordinary human speech. Steve Parsons, one of Britain's best paranormal investigators, and a helpful advisor to me in the writing of this chapter, summarizes the odd characteristics of EVP speech recorded on tape. When played back,

> The voice-entities speak very rapidly, in a mixture of languages.... They speak in a definite rhythm, which seems to be forced upon them.... The rhythmic mode of speech imposes a shortened, telegram-style

phrase or sentence.... grammatical rules are frequently abandoned and neologisms abound.

Occasionally the voices try to explain why they sound so weird. Professor Senkowski wrote: "We have been told that they send short pulses containing long contents of which we receive only a limited part." Here is an example, spoken to Dr. Cardoso from Rio do Tempo: "We are all dead... Rio do Tempo... We are all dead... We are the dead from Tempo, Aunt, Father, November." November? Serious researchers suspect that this strange eruption of speech doesn't do justice to the speaker's intent. Cardoso tells us that Rio do Tempo is working as hard at their end to make their thoughts understandable as we are at ours. She wonders if we hear the words they specifically choose or only their thoughts. If it is their thoughts, this could "explain the odd sentence structure often found in ITC voices, a characteristic that has been a topic of discussion in almost every book on ITC research." She surmises that their thoughts "could have a different grammatical expression from formal, deliberate speech."

Cardoso is especially impressed by moments when she can overhear behind-the-scenes conversation which may include several voices—voices not addressing her but talking *about* her:

> At times they can even be heard making surprising comments to each other such as, 'It is Anabella asking about the making of the voices again,' or similar comments about other issues and then, without a pause, we can hear them uninterruptedly talking to each other again.... Usually, when this strange situation happens, the voices sound more natural and often are not distorted, but they can also appear and disappear suddenly.

Another challenge for the serious ITC experimenter is the reluctance of the voices to provide requested information. Cardoso warns us "not to forget that, as other researchers and I have reported elsewhere, the communicators themselves have repeatedly informed us that they are not allowed to reply to certain questions." She reports that there are times when a voice different from the one speaking to her breaks in and closes the conversation with a remark like, "It is over." At other times "an imposing voice will suddenly break into the communication to direct the trend of the conversation." Is there a danger that we can be told more than we should know about conditions on the Other

Side? David Fontana finds himself wondering from time to time if "the Almighty may have decreed that we are never going to receive the final element of proof for which survival researchers have been looking."

But there are other explanations for these difficulties. Cardoso tells us that the communicators "have repeatedly said that the state of mind of the experimenter is of importance for the success of the communication." She believes from experience, and from what she is told, that "a few minutes of silence in a state of calm detachment are advisable before the taping session," and that a lack of seriousness, sincerity, or collectedness on the part of the experimenter will scuttle the communication before it starts. The communicators "seem to be constantly aware of our intentions and goals," she explains. Moreover,

> A previous interaction of some kind between communicators and experimenters seems to be essential, even though this interaction may be a difficult and time-consuming process, producing only poor results over a number of years before there is any discernible improvement in voice reception.

Another explanation for failure is intentional interference by negative forces. Rio do Tempo once told Cardoso, "It is negative groups in our world that do not want humans to know that life continues."

But perhaps, after all, the main reason we have such a hard time communicating through electronic instruments is that they lack the refinement and precision needed for clear, unbroken, extensive communication; or that we simply don't know how best to do it; or that no mere instrument will ever be up to the task. Both Dr. Cardoso and Steve Parsons go into detail about how to get the best results. Cardoso tells the would-be experimenter, for example, how far to place the microphone from the radio and how high to turn up the volume of white noise. And Parsons tells how to "reduce handling noise and other vibrations" that might interfere with the voice trying to come through: "simply place the recorder on a piece of sponge or foam rubber." And so forth. Even the voices themselves are of limited help. When Cardoso asked Rio do Tempo "why their voices were sometimes very clear, other times distorted, and on yet other occasions inaudible, their interesting reply was, 'We don't know.'"

But this lack of knowledge does not detract from the evidential quality of the voices. Do they belong to spirits? Do they prove that we will live on after death just as they apparently have? Do they give us one more stick to add to our bundle? In all that we have surveyed up until now in this chapter, what stands out?

First, the voices explicitly say over and over that they belong to deceased humans. But can we trust them? Some skeptics have proposed that they are probably just "stray radio transmissions misinterpreted by listeners," but this objection is plainly ridiculous. The staccato style of speech, the odd sentence structure, and, most important, the conversational give-and-take between experimenter and communicator rule it out absolutely. Well then, perhaps the voices are simply explained by hoax, says the skeptic. If so, there are tens of thousands of hoaxers all over the world, and they are earning nothing for their efforts. Moreover, the reputations of the main ITC pioneers have remained unblemished. Dr. Cardoso is one of these. Recall that on two occasions David Fontana, one of the world's leading parapsychologists, stayed in her home and was on the constant lookout for trickery of some kind. After checking the house to make sure there was no confederate working with her to deceive him, he watched her converse with communicators in Portuguese. There was no doubt in his mind that they were responding to questions she put to them, and he understood much of what was said. Furthermore:

> Dr. Cardoso herself is regarded by all who know her as a person of unimpeachable integrity, and the notion that a high-ranking diplomat in her position would compromise herself by faking supposed spirit communications is out of the question. There can be no doubt that the recordings made by her and to which I have listened are genuine.

Another possibility, occasionally raised by critics of ITC, is that the voices are caused by psychokinesis (PK), or the unconscious creation of the voices by the experimenters themselves. Hans Bender, one of Europe's most respected parapsychologists in the latter part of the last century, believed that experimenters, hoping to get results, unconsciously impressed words on the tape that were later taken to be the voices of spirits. Bender's primary target was the same Friedrich Jürgenson we met earlier. He was a Swedish documentary filmmaker and author of *Radio Communications with the Dead* (1967), and one of the most respected early pioneers in ITC. Fontana finds little merit in Bender's thesis:

> ... the notion that Jürgenson had psychokinetic abilities powerful

enough to produce sustained, repeated, and often coherent voices on audio tapes, although these abilities had hitherto failed to revealed themselves during his many years work with audio tapes as a documentary film maker, may seem to many people harder to swallow than the spirit communication hypothesis.

Fontana's judgment seems on the mark to me. And it is supported by his own observations while staying in Dr. Cardoso's houses, with permission to move about them without restriction. He reports: "While staying in the house I have frequently heard voices from the radios at unexpected times of the day or night that are so loud and seemingly insistent that I have entered the empty studio in the hope of hearing communications." One wonders what Bender would say about this? There was no one present to psychokinetically create the voices. Bender's thesis strikes me as farfetched at best.

Another attempt to explain away spirit communication, and thus afterlife, is the alien hypothesis. Are extraterrestrials behind the voices? It is possible, but, again, what is more likely—that aliens are trying to communicate to us, or that the dead are? Cardoso believes in the reality of aliens (because the voices say that aliens are real) but argues against them as the origin of the communications. She says:

> ... why would the aliens tell us they are deceased people? What would be their purpose in doing so?... And in view of the high ethical teachings behind many ITC communications, why would they wish, nevertheless, to deceive us in this way?

The alien hypothesis cannot be ruled out, but it seems relatively outlandish compared to the more obvious thesis that it is the dead who are talking to us. As we've seen, they speak to us in other ways as well—through mediums and the nearly dead.

But the most often heard argument against ITC is that the voices aren't really voices at all, but fantasies projected on random noise by experimenters eager to find meaning where there is none. The psychologist, James Alcock, speaks for almost all of his profession with this predictable dismissal: "Electronic Voice Phenomena are the products of hope and expectation; the claims wither away under the light of scientific scrutiny." One wonders if Alcock has ever listened to any of the voices he scorns. They can be found online at Dr. Cardoso's website; the voices emerging out of the hissing white noise are unmistakable;

they are not imagined. Nor was Professor Senkowski's message from his deceased wife, Adelheid. Here is his account:

> Sitting beside the switched-on radio I said: 'Hast du eine Mitteilung für mich, liebe Adelheid?' (Have you a message for me, dear Adelheid?) And a clear female voice without noisy background immediately answered word by word, 'Hallo - hier - Adelheid - bitte.' (Hello - here - Adelheid - please.) I did not hear it directly from the loudspeaker in spite of the fact that it was a <u>loud</u> voice on the tape (EVP voice).

Smug dismissals of the thousands of recordings as "unreal" or "unscientific" are ridiculous. What's behind this attitude is fear—fear of the paradigm shift that would have to occur for the voices to be taken seriously. Again we come face to face with the prevalent materialism of high-profile scientists and technicians. There is room for debate over the source of the voices, but to deny their existence is to follow the example of the ostrich.

ITC research, for all its mysteries and confounding challenges, represents a new phase in humanity's attempt to prove the existence of an afterlife. Voices on tape are data that can be heard or seen by anyone and have an objective quality about them quite different from, say, the mind of a medium, where there is the ever-present danger of unconscious fabrication or "coloring" by the medium's mind. Moreover, they are often repeatable. Dr. Cardoso puts it well:

> Instrumental Transcommunication, for the first time in history, offers the possibility of repeatable experiments highly indicative of the survival of physical death of all forms of consciousness. At present, although ITC phenomena cannot always be received on demand, it is, nevertheless, clear that they repeat themselves frequently all over the world under conditions that include a range of similar characteristics.

On the other hand, we learn far more about the ins and outs of life in the world of spirit from mediums than from ITC, though professional experimenters hope to change this. Why might this be? Do spirits have an easier time projecting their thoughts into a living human brain than into an inert radio or television set? I suspect so. And certainly deceased spirits have more in common with our conscious selves than with an electrical device. Greater ease of transmission from spirit to medium might be the reason for the rich syntax and in-depth descriptions reaching us through authentic mediums, as opposed to the choppy, truncated expressions reaching us through instruments.

Be that as it may, ITC is one more stick to add to our bundle, and one that could conceivably grow in importance as better transmission is achieved. Who knows? ITC might eventually evolve into the most respected of all the evidences pointing with force to the reality of an afterlife. This depends, say Cardoso and others at the top of this strange and exhilarating profession, on our ability to develop a technology that allows our spirit friends to come through with accuracy and ease.

9.

TERMINAL LUCIDITY

An elderly woman never speaks, no longer recognizes her loved ones when they come to visit, and shows no expression. By the looks of her, she is a human vegetable. And she's been this way for over a year. Her brain's cerebral cortex and hippocampus—necessary for memory, thought, language, and normal consciousness—are severely shrunk. Her brain bears little resemblance to a healthy one.

Yet something utterly astonishing is about to happen. As reported by both the nursing staff of her care unit and her family members, "Unexpectedly, she calls her daughter and thanks her for everything. She has a phone conversation with her grandchildren, exchanges kindness and warmth. She says farewell and shortly thereafter dies."

Similar cases have been scattered side notes in the medical literature, but recently a small body of researchers, such as Bruce Greyson, Professor of Psychiatry and Neurobehavioral Sciences at the University of Virginia, and biologist Michael Nahm in Freiburg, Germany, have begun to take a careful look at the phenomenon and agreed to call it terminal lucidity, or TL. Professor Alexander Batthyany, who teaches cognitive science at the University of Vienna, is currently running a large-scale study of the phenomenon—-the first of its kind. He is sending out detailed questionnaires to caregivers of Alzheimer's victims, mostly nurses and medical doctors, and as the questionnaires trickle in, new mysteries arise as fast as older ones are clarified. The case cited above comes from Batthyany's database.

Almost all brain scientists have assumed up until now that a severely damaged brain makes normal cognition impossible. But Batthyany's preliminary results, presented at the 2014 IANDS (International Association for Near-Death Study) Annual Congress in Newport, California, suggests that normal cognition, or lucidity, does occur in spite of a severely damaged brain—not often, but in about 5-10% of Alzheimer's cases. And only when death is very near. This has led him to wonder how terminal lucidity—which he describes as "close to a miracle, given what we know about brain function and cognition"—can occur. What is actually going on during those amazing moments? We know that there is no observable change in the brain—the cerebral cortex doesn't suddenly grow billions of new neurons—so what accounts for TL?

Conventional brain science has no explanation. It has long assumed that as the brain goes, so goes the mind; for the brain is what gives rise to the mind, it claims. The return of mental clarity and memory in a brain ravaged by Alzheimer's is not supposed to happen. Yet it does in some cases.

This has given rise to some unorthodox speculation. Could it be that the conventional wisdom is wrong? Is it possible that the mind's sudden and short-lived return to normalcy just before death is brought about, not by some inexplicable surge in brain functioning, but by the mind disengaging itself from the brain? What if the brain does not give rise to the mind, as commonly thought? What if the mind uses the brain as its organ? What if the mind of an Alzheimer's victim is like the sun in eclipse, and the moon obscuring the sun like the sick brain? Batthyany is far from claiming this, but he does wonder about it. Indeed the analogy of eclipse is his.

To put it differently, it is possible that the conscious self—the thinking, feeling being that we are—is very much intact when we are stricken by Alzheimer's, but has been hampered from expressing itself in the normal way because of its confinement in a diseased brain. In the early stages of the disease, Alzheimer's victims are often painfully aware that they can't formulate their thoughts; it's like trying to formulate a message on a computer when it has a virus. There is nothing wrong with you, the user of the computer, but your message comes out scrambled or incoherent because you're stuck with a faulty instrument. And if you can't get it fixed, you might give up trying to communicate altogether. But the onset of death alters the situation. You begin to peel away from the sick brain and suddenly find yourself able to remember, think, and communicate normally.

How this communication once free from the brain is accomplished is of course mysterious—but no more so, Batthyany says, than communication through it. Batthyany's research is in its very early stages. He hopes that more questionnaires, thousands more, will bring more clarity and tip the scales in one direction or another.

Batthyany is aware of research on the near-death experience and deathbed visions. On the surface both suggest a view of the self that he is contemplating here—that the conscious self is an autonomous agent working through a material brain. Like TL, these visions take place, he told me by email, "when materialistically speaking one would be least likely to expect such complex coherence and often deeply meaningful experiences." He is not ready, however, to claim that his research into terminal lucidity points to survival beyond death. But it does suggest a crucial distinction between the brain, which obviously dies, and the self—the user of the brain—which might not. At the moment his position is that "more studies are needed, that our study is ongoing, and that it is far too early to draw any strong conclusions other than that TL does occur, even if only rarely, and that it is a solid mystery which needs to be studied in more detail."

In the meantime, cases of terminal lucidity continue to occur, and there are lessons to be learned for all of us. One of Batthyany's respondents confessed how she used to consider her advanced Alzheimer's patients "human vegetables." A single instance of TL changed her outlook completely: "Had you seen what I saw, you could understand that dementia can affect the soul but not destroy it. I only wish I had known this earlier."

When we broaden our horizon, we discover that terminal lucidity is not unique to Alzheimer's patients but occurs in other conditions. In 2007 Dr. Scott Haig, an assistant clinical professor of orthopedic surgery at the Columbia University College of Physicians and Surgeons, described a case in a lung cancer patient, David, whose brain had been destroyed by the cancer following metastasis. The term "terminal lucidity" hadn't been invented yet (it wouldn't be until 2009), but what he described in *Time* Magazine fit the paradigm perfectly:

> [David] stopped speaking, then moving…. The cerebral machine [the brain] that talked and wondered, winked and sang, the machine that remembered jokes and birthdays and where the big fish hid on hot

days, was nearly gone, replaced by lumps of haphazardly growing gray stuff. Gone with that machine seemed David as well. No expression, no response to anything we did to him. As far as I could tell, he was just not there.

But just before his death, with his family surrounding him, he became lucid. A nurse on the floor witnessed the event:

He woke up, you know, doctor—just after you left—and said goodbye to them all. Like I'm talkin' to you right here. Like a miracle. He talked to them and patted them and smiled for about five minutes. Then he went out again, and he passed in the hour.

Dr. Haig didn't use unscientific language like "miracle" to portray what had happened, but he didn't back away from saying what really happened either. He described David's mind as "uncloaked." It had somehow loosened itself from the brain:

...it wasn't David's brain that woke him up to say goodbye that Friday. His brain had already been destroyed. Tumor metastases don't simply occupy space and press on things, leaving a whole brain. The metastases actually replace tissue. Where that gray stuff grows, the brain is just not there.... What woke my patient that Friday was simply his mind, forcing its way through a broken brain, a father's final act to comfort his family.

If consciousness, or the "mind," is separated from the brain at death, then the mind is free to go its own way. The dead brain has no claim on it.

Some of the most striking cases of terminal lucidity take us back to the 19th and early 20th centuries, when, surprisingly, there was far more readiness to investigate the phenomenon than in the later 20th. No one has delved into these old cases more thoroughly than Dr. Nahm. Not only did he invent the term "terminal lucidity"; his lengthy historical survey of TL written for *The Journal of Near-Death Studies* is, at present, the gold standard for anyone interested in TL. His analysis of its causes are even more important. (As of this writing, TL is such a new field that no one has yet written a book devoted exclusively to it.)

Here is a typical case, from 1921. A man had been housed in an insane asylum (the term used for a mental hospital in earlier times) for many years. One day the man's brother got a telegram from the asylum's director, saying that his brother wanted to speak to him.

He immediately visited his brother and was astonished to find him in a perfectly normal mental state. On leaving again, the director of the asylum decently informed the visitor that his brother's mental clarity is an almost certain sign of his approaching death. Indeed, the patient died within a short time. Subsequently, an autopsy of the brain was performed, to which [the brother] was allowed to attend. It revealed that the brain was entirely suppurated and that this condition must have been present for a long time.

The author of the article asks: "With what, then, did this brainsick person think intelligibly again during the last days of his life?"

A more eerie case, from 1926, follows. A farmer's wife had spent the last eight years of her life in an asylum, where she lived in what seemed like an imbecilic stupor:

Usually, the woman just stared in front of her; and – if at all – uttered only detestable swear words. When visited by the doctor or the priest, she displayed an odd virtuosity in successfully spitting on their shoes. One day, she began to converse rationally with her caretaker and apologized from deep within her heart for her bad behaviour. Broken and remorseful, she affirmed she was not able to behave in any other way since she had been forced to act like this. It was her utmost concern whether she would be forgiven for these and other sins. When the priest arrived, he handed her the requested Lord's Supper. The next morning, she died in peace.

On thinking over this case, Dr. Nahm felt it resembled an earlier case in which the patient, during a period of TL just before death, described his long illness, from which he was momentarily freed, as a "bad dream." Nahm suspects that the cause of TL in such cases is probably not a loosening of consciousness from a sick brain, but a freeing of consciousness from a malevolent spiritual presence controlling its victim's mind. This shows, he claims, how difficult it is to assign a common cause to all cases of TL—a point to which we will soon return when framing an argument against materialism.

The most extraordinary early case of terminal lucidity comes from Friedrich Happich, the director of a German asylum from 1913 up to the mid-1930s. Peter Ringger summarizes the event:

One of the most disabled patients of Happich's asylum was Käthe. From birth on, she was seriously retarded and never learned to speak a single word. She could only utter animal-like voices; her bodily abilities did not exceed uncontrolled spasms. It never seemed that she took notice of what was happening around her even for a second. One day, Happich was called to immediately visit Käthe by a physician and psychiatrist of the asylum, Dr. Wittweber. Käthe was ill with tuberculosis and she was about to die. When entering the room, Happich was stunned. He continues: "We did not believe our eyes and ears. Käthe, who never spoke one word, entirely mentally disabled from birth on, sang the dying songs to herself. Specifically, she sang 'Where does the soul find its home, its peace? Peace, peace, heavenly peace!' over and over again. For half an hour she sang. Then, she quietly died. Her face, up to then so stultified, was transfigured and spiritualized. Like myself and the present nurse, the physician had tears in his eyes. He stated repeatedly: 'I cannot explain this in medical terms. If demanded, I can prove by autopsy that ... from an anatomical perspective, thinking could not have been possible.'"

Nahm is especially impressed by this case, for "there was no return of previously available faculties but, rather, the emergence of a qualitatively new bodily skill, namely speaking. To my knowledge, no materialistic theory of psychology or neurology to date could account convincingly" for such a case: "brain physiology is of only minor importance."

Nahm looks to the research of British neurologist John Lorber, whose work with hydrocephalic patients (patients with "water on the brain") in the second half of the 20th century underscored the independence of mind from brain function. Nahm writes:

After performing more than 600 scans on hydrocephalic patients, Lorber put forward [in 1983] the provocative question, "Is your brain really necessary?" He found that about 30 individuals had a global IQ greater than 100 – despite cerebrospinal fluid instead of brain tissue filling 95% or more of their crania. Lorber loved citing the story of a student of mathematics whose global IQ was 126, his verbal IQ even reaching 143. In his case, "instead of the normal 4.5 centimeter thickness of brain tissue between the ventricles and the cortical surface, there was just a thin layer of mantle measuring a millimeter or so.... The boy has virtually no brain."

Hardly any brain, yet full consciousness. Severely shrunk, damaged, or destroyed brain, yet normal consciousness during TL. On the other hand, psychiatry reveals almost no difference between the brains of apparently possessed or severely psychotic individuals and those of normal people. How can this be? It can be only if the brain and the mind are two different things.

One of the strangest, most unexpected discoveries in recent years has been the sudden burst of activity in the brains of dying individuals who have been removed from life-support machines. Minutes after removal, when the heart stops beating and blood pressure drops to zero (cardiac death), "the BIS number [indicating brain activity] spiked to approximately 80 in all three [hopelessly brain-damaged] cases, and remained there for 30 to 90 seconds. The number then abruptly returned to near zero," according to Drs. Stuart Hameroff and Deepak Chopra. The question remains: what caused the brain's sudden activity when the heart was dead and not functioning? Hameroff and Chopra speculate that it might be related to the soul leaving the body in a spasm of freedom. But no one can be sure.

I bring this up because of its similarity to cases of TL in dying people with damaged brains. Is their lucidity caused by their soul disengaging from those brains? And in cases of dying patients whose life-support is removed, might that 30-to-90-second surge in brain activity be accompanied by consciousness? It wouldn't surprise me, but we can never know, for they don't come back to tell us.

Terminal Lucidity is not the exclusive preserve of doctors and parapsychologists. Nurses, especially hospice personnel, commonly report such cases. So do ordinary folk who describe their experiences after reading about such cases in online articles. Here is an example, and a fitting way to end this chapter from just such a person:

> I read this article because I've experienced this myself with my own father many years ago. He had a devastating stroke when I was 14, and was severely brain damaged and paralyzed. He didn't know me, or anyone else afterwards. Right before he died when I was 16, he spoke to us (Mom, me, sister) and knew things he hadn't known for 2 years, like who we were, and what had happened to him, and he was now ready to go. It was pretty incredible, and he died 2 days after he had this "awakening" that had lasted for about 20 minutes.

10.

PHILOSOPHY AND THE AFTERLIFE

For many years academic philosophers have been waging a campaign, often stealthily, sometimes openly, against the age-old doctrine of the soul that most Americans over 30 were raised on. This soul doctrine is known as dualism. It is the belief that matter and spirit, or body and soul, are different kinds of reality and can exist independently of each other. It gives scope for the satellite belief in an afterlife—the body dies, but the soul, being a different sort of thing, escapes death and goes on. I've been watching this campaign with increasing concern as college freshmen watch their family traditions come under fire from philosophy professors they can't match wits with. Does a materialist philosophy that denies the existence of the soul lead to pessimism in the here-and-now? It's a fair question.

According to most of these professors, the active brain produces consciousness. In academic philosophical circles this position is sometimes called *property dualism:* consciousness is a property of the brain. It has several versions, but what they all share is that without a functioning brain, there can be no conscious experience—or *qualia*, to use the current academic jargon. That means that when you're dead, that's the end of you—unless God works a miracle (as a few Christian philosophers claim).

Property dualism isn't the "real deal" that philosophers like me support, and I regret the term's use. To distinguish the real deal from this pretender, philosophers have come up with the term *substance dualism*—the dualism I will be defending here. It holds that the soul is nonphysical; we can't see, hear, or touch it. But it's no less real than the physical body with which it is allied. Its nature is to *be aware*, to *be conscious*. Moreover, it can exist even where there is no physical stuff at all, and exist more intensely, more purely. It's not a property of an active physical brain, and it's not caused by the brain. The brain doesn't *cause* the soul; it helps it. It helps it navigate through physical space. It's the partner the soul dances with for as long as it lives on a physical planet. To avoid confusion, I will use an older term for property dualism: epiphenomenalism. An epiphenomenon is an unexpected side-effect of something else, in this instance a living brain. An epiphenomenalist, then, is a materialist who claims the brain *produces* consciousness, while a dualist (we'll drop the word *substance* from here on) claims it *facilitates* consciousness.

Dualism holds that the invisible mind, or self, or soul interacts with the brain in some intimate and mysterious way but is not reducible to it. An analogy which I often use in my university classes might be helpful. Consider the way sunlight interacts with a prism. White light flows in one side and comes out the other broken up into the colors of the rainbow—a process known as refraction. The brain is like the prism, refracting the light of the self: The pure consciousness of the self is broken up into the myriad experiences of everyday life. As long as the prism remains intact, it refracts white light as intended—just as a healthy brain collaborates with the self in the production of normal conscious states. Note that the light is not identical to the prism, just as the self is not identical to the brain. Yet they work in a seamless harmony, the prism making refraction possible.

The self does depend on its brain—a healthy one at that—for its proper functioning for as long as it is locked in interaction with the brain. Try chipping a prism and see what happens. The light doesn't refract as intended. Damage a brain, and the self can't think coherently, if at all. Destroy a brain, and then what? Does the light stop shining because the prism is shattered? No. It just doesn't shine through the prism anymore.

Dualists believe that when the brain stops working, the self, like the sun, keeps on shining—only not through a physical brain. It shines elsewhere. And that which shines is who we are.

But is there any evidence of this?

The evidence for a robust, full-bodied dualism like the one sketched here is available and impressive. But it's seldom presented in philosophy classes, where physicalist assumptions about the nature of the self are rarely seriously questioned. This monopoly on human thought on so serious a subject is, to say the least, unfair to students. It leaves the impression that there is no purpose to life other than what we invent for ourselves, that there is no afterlife and thus no victory over a dreaded death, and that there is no ultimate accountability for the decisions we make in life.

I would reluctantly endorse these unhappy conclusions if that was where the evidence pointed. But it doesn't. If philosophers would allow themselves to study with care the full range of parapsychological phenomena—what we've been looking at up to this point–many would tiptoe away from their too-hasty conclusions and perhaps approach the soul-body question in a more balanced way. Others would at least be puzzled.

But there is a different kind of evidence for the soul, one less empirical. It grows out of a careful study of the very nature of consciousness; we'll call this study the phenomenological approach. When you turn inward and catch yourself thinking a thought or experiencing an emotion, what is its nature? Does the thought have a shape you can see? Does the emotion make a sound you can hear? Does it have a texture you can touch? Does it have a scent or taste? Does it have volume and take up space? Is it to the left or right of something? What is its weight? Its color? Is the feeling of hunger—not the cause of hunger such as an empty stomach, but the actual feeling—distinguishable from the feeling of being full that we have after a hearty meal? We know it is, but we can't describe the difference in physical terms. And what about our emotions of anger, confusion, happiness, or excitement? Does each have its own unique shape and color that allows us to distinguish them from each other? And our ideas don't have physical attributes either. But if they have no physical attributes, are they therefore unreal? On the contrary, they are the most real things about us. Our interior life is who we are in a far more basic way than the body we see in the mirror. If we are forced to decide which is more real, more basic, more essential, the body or our consciousness, there is no contest.

What does this little meditation have to do with the soul? By definition the soul is nonphysical, as we have seen. Its nature is to be conscious. It gives us our sense of self and all the experiences that go with the self. But you can't see it. Now here is the question that we ought to be asking ourselves at this point. Is it more likely that all this non-physical experience—all the mental and emotional events of our inner life—is the property of a physical body, in particular a physical brain, or of a nonphysical soul? In everyone's experience it's far more common to see effects emerging from causes that are of the same nature than from causes that are strikingly dissimilar. What does a physical brain have in common with our thoughts and feelings? You can cut the brain with a knife, pickle it, even eat it. The brain is made of meat; if it can think and feel, then we have to come to terms with the awkward truth that meat can think and feel. And that strikes most of us as very strange. It feels strange because there is nothing at all meaty about our interior life, our thoughts and feelings. It feels much less strange to think of our interior life as coming from that part of us that is *not* meaty—that which we call the soul.

No one should pretend, however, that dualism is without problems of its own, and materialists never stop pointing them out. We need to look at the materialist critique in more detail. In spite of first appearances, is it possible the materialist gives a better account of how consciousness arises than the dualist?

The materialist critique goes like this: Substances that are as radically different as matter and non-matter, or body and a supposed soul, have no purchase on each other; they have no way of influencing each other. You might as well try to remove a smell with a backhoe, or fix a flat tire with a wish. Yet, as we all know, our body works as a smoothly functioning unit. How can this be? In particular, how can a soul cause anything to happen in the material brain or be influenced in turn by that brain? It cannot, says the materialist. Thus the soul has to go. The well-known philosopher, Colin McGinn, puts the case well:

> Causation in the material world works by energy transfer of some sort: transfer of motion, electrical energy, gravitational force. But pure consciousness could not give off energies of these kinds, so how does it cause changes in anything? How does it reach out and touch something? What mediates its alleged causal powers?

Materialists believe they have a better way of accounting for consciousness. Their "solutions" come in many versions, but ultimately they all fall under one of two headings: (1) reductive (or hard) materialism and (2) epiphenomenalism, a kind of soft materialism sometimes referred to as property dualism, as we saw above.

Reductive materialists hold that consciousness or conscious experience is ultimately nothing more than brain activity. John Searle, though not himself a materialist of this kind, summarizes the position: ". . . mental states are just brain states. For example, to be in pain is just to have your C-fibers stimulated." Physicalists of this kind are not epiphenomenalists. Whereas epiphenomenalists hold that brain activity *gives rise* to conscious experience, reductive materialists hold that brain activity *is* conscious experience. The color red that we all experience, they say, is nothing more than a very specific kind of electrochemical brain event. True, they admit, brain activity does not seem like experience, but experiences are deceiving. The kind of introspection that reveals a certain kind of phenomenology—like the color red—is not to be trusted. First-person reporting of this nature is not conducive to truth. Only third-person reporting of what is actually happening in the brain can reveal the true nature of consciousness.

The strength of reductive materialism is its supposed appeal to the scientific method. If what we call consciousness can be deprived of its mysterious character, if it can be embroidered into the physical fabric of the universe and deprived of its apparent immateriality, then it will deserve to take its place alongside the myriad physical things and processes that the physical sciences can make good sense of, and it will be only a matter of time before the workings of the mind will be fully understood. Most if not all mystery will have been removed, and mind-body theorists will at last be able to rest on their laurels and be done with dualism for good.

The main weakness of reductive materialism is that its identification of physical brain states with conscious experience is utterly bizarre. Even Daniel Dennett, one of the theory's stoutest present-day supporters, admits that making a case for it "appears to be a trick with mirrors . . . counterintuitive, hard to swallow, initially outrageous." He and his colleagues are of course undaunted and build their cases impressively, but many of their peers remain unconvinced. Thomas Nagel, David Chalmers, Frank Jackson, and McGinn are just a few. Jackson writes:

> Tell me everything physical there is to tell about what is going on in a living brain, the kind of states, their functional role, their relation to what goes on at other times and in other brains, and so on and so forth, and be I as clever as can be in fitting it all together, you won't have told me about the hurtfulness of pains, the itchiness of itches,

pangs of jealousy, or about the characteristic experience of tasting a lemon, smelling a rose, hearing a loud noise or seeing the sky.

For Chalmers there is an "explanatory gap" between brain function-ing and experience, "and we need an explanatory bridge to cross it." Nagel agrees. In his famous essay "What Is It Like to Be a Bat?" Nagel says that the "idea of how a mental and a physical term might refer to the same thing is lacking, and the usual analogies . . . fail to supply it." He concludes: "If we acknowledge that a physical theory of mind must account for the subjective character of experience, we must admit that no presently available conception gives us a clue how this could be done."

Reductive materialists are often scornful of epiphenomenalists, but at least epiphenomenalism is intelligible. Epiphenomenalists can't tell you how experience arises from brain chemistry, but at least they don't ask you to *identify* the two. They don't insist that a person's ex-perience of the color red is identical to an electrochemical event in the squashy gray brain.

Let me confess that I lose all patience with reductive materialism, a position I regard as absurd. Will a gentler form of materialism account for the irreducible extraordinariness of conscious experience any better?

McGinn and Chalmers, though differing from each other in some ways, share the following commitments: They forcefully reject reduc-tive materialism, yet they will have nothing to do with dualism (or what they call substance dualism). Because of the first commitment, they part company with their hard-line materialist brethren. Because of the second, they reject belief in such things as higher ("spiritual") beings and worlds, and they do not believe that we have, or are, "spiritual" souls. And, of course, there is no afterlife.

We have space to look at the soft materialism of only one of them, McGinn. He is quite clear he does not know how consciousness is pro-duced, but he is sure that the process is natural, that is, that it does not involve anything like a soul. This is how he puts it:

My thesis is that consciousness depends upon an unknowable natural property of the brain. What this means is that I am not going to try to reduce consciousness to those mundane known properties of neurons that [reductive] materialists hope to get by with. But neither am I going to conceive of consciousness as something apart from the brain, something with no further analysis or explanation. Consciousness is rooted in the brain via some natural property of brain tissue, but it is not explicable in terms of electrochemical processes of the familiar kind. I shall argue that it is the very unknowability of this property that generates all our perplexities. The [reductive] materialists are right to think that it is some property of the brain that is responsible for consciousness, but they are wrong in the kind of brain property they select. The dualists are right to doubt that the brain as currently conceived can explain the mind, but they are wrong to infer that no brain property can do the job.

McGinn is a soft materialist: he believes the brain gives rise to consciousness, but how this happens is unknowable and utterly mysterious. (He calls himself a "Mysterian.") Correlating neuronal activity with different conscious states is easy, he believes; any brain mechanic can learn to do that. "All I have said is that the philosophical mind-body problem cannot be solved: the problem of explaining how brains can give rise to consciousness in the first place." His view is typical of most soft materialists.

I admire McGinn's humility. He admits he has no clue how consciousness is produced by the brain. But he leaves us disappointed, with only mystery to offer. I find myself wondering why he should be so determined to rule out soul as the cause? Is it because he can't see it? But he can't see a thought or an emotion either, yet they are real to him. So while McGinn avoids a mistake, he shies away from a solution. He fails to develop a theory that gives a minimally intelligible account of where consciousness comes from and how it works.

We are now in a better position to take stock. Clearly the brain is profoundly involved in our thinking and feeling and willing—in every phase of consciousness: no dualist disputes this. Yet the brain belongs entirely to the physical world. Take it out of its skull and you can weigh it and measure it. Not so the thoughts that seem to come forth from it. As we have agreed, they have no weight, no volume, no texture, no density, no shape, no color, no exact location. They are not high or low, short or long, heavy or light, dark or pale. How they arise from the brain's electrochemistry is "the hard problem," as Chalmers famously put it.

Dualists say that the best way to account for thoughts with these characteristics is to postulate a source that is like them: a source as nonphysical as they are, call it soul or self or mind. Whatever its name, it is the seat and source of consciousness. And it is radically different from matter as we know it. And because it's radically different, it need not share the same fate as the body when it dies.

So the question again arises: How do immaterial states of consciousness and the material brain affect each other, as they most certainly seem to? No one knows, but dualism has two immediate advantages over materialism: First, it is consistent with everyday experience—I speak of "my body," something I use and control, something that is not quite me but is intimately connected to me—I like to call it the most intimate part of my environment. In addition it has a remedy for the heart's deepest needs. The eminent materialist philosopher John Searle admits this. "Dualism," he says, "not only is consistent with the most obvious interpretation of our experiences but it also satisfies a very deep urge we have for survival." Second, there is all that paranormal evidence. A brain can't leave its body, but an immaterial self, or soul, apparently can. A brain can't know what another brain miles away, or even a person lacking a physical brain altogether, is communicating, but there is nothing we know about a self that makes either event impossible. A brain can't work after it dies, but there is no law telling us an immaterial structure—like a self or soul or mind—must cease to work just because the brain it formerly interacted with can't. Dualism has a lot going for it. It is time for establishment philosophy to take another look.

But the scandal of dualism's failure to show how two incompatible substances, body and soul, can interact so harmoniously is still with us. Can we come up with something better than dualism?

There is another way to explain the relation between body and soul that is potentially helpful. Instead of describing human beings as made up of two radically contrasting substances, it collapses them into a single substance with widely differing qualities and aptitudes: it posits not two different substances but many grades of a single substance. Ultimately it is not dualistic, but monistic. Let's agree to call this theory "Qualified Monism."

This monistic theory of reality will help us remove the scandal of incompatible substances that tarnish traditional dualism. The great Swiss psychotherapist Carl Jung suggests why. In 1946 he wrote:

> Since psyche [or soul] and matter are contained in one and the same world, and moreover are in continuous contact with one another and ultimately rest on irrepresentable, transcendental factors, it is not only possible but fairly probable, even, that psyche and matter are two different aspects of one and the same thing.

Like me, Jung is uncomfortable with the bipolar thinking of conventional dualists, even more so with the reductive theories of contemporary materialists, whom he refers to as "weaker minds" unduly impressed by "the spirit of the age." Jung is staking out a middle ground between these two extremes, and so am I.

Building on Jung's insight, let us think of reality—all of it—as composed of a single kind of substance. We can use the Greek word *ousia* (often translated as substance) to name it. This *ousia* has innumerable grades of grossness and subtlety, ranging from the utterly dense stuff of what we call lifeless matter like a piece of coal to the inconceivably subtle "stuff" of the human soul. The qualitative difference between these two extremes is impossible to exaggerate, yet both are expressions of only one substance, one *ousia*. There is nothing novel about this view of reality. We find it in Spinoza, for example, and we find it in the ancient Stoics. It's attractive to us here because—and this is the key point—it's a lot easier to account for interaction between two things as different as mind and brain if they are both ultimately made of the same *ousia*, than if they are made of substances that have absolutely nothing in common.

This solution might seem strange at first, but that's probably because we have assumed that if something can't be sensed it must be completely immaterial and therefore nothing like things that are material. Many of us grew up hearing that our bodies were material and our souls spiritual, that is, completely lacking any kind of matter. But when did we ever stop to ask what our souls were made of? They must be made of something, or they wouldn't exist. And that is what we are calling *ousia*, the primal substance that gives everything that is, its being. This *ousia*, we are suggesting, is the universal "reality stuff." And consciousness might be made of *ousia* so refined and ethereal that we cannot sense it, while material things are made of *ousia* so dense that we can. But it's all the same *ousia*. If so, all reality is of a piece—as Jung suspected—so the scandal of soul-body interaction has been considerably eased.

I can't say whether traditional dualism or something like the qualified monism developed here is the correct theory, but this I do know: When some people are having an out-of-body experience, they feel they are out of their gross body but are still somehow embodied—they don't feel naked. They retain their sense of self and continue to think and sense a subtler "astral" environment. And if they are blind, they discover to their amazement that in this new environment they can see. So the self, if we are to take NDErs at their word, interacts not only with our presently visible body but with an inner body (with its subtle inner brain) that is presently invisible to us. And there is nothing to rule out interaction with additional invisible bodies of varying material texture, from ghostly to indescribably ethereal. Whether the NDEr's knowing self is material in some exquisitely subtle sense or completely immaterial is not discussed in any of the NDE literature I've been exposed to, and certainly it has not been resolved in this chapter, though I prefer the monistic account.

This chapter would be incomplete if I didn't say something about the AI, or Artificial Intelligence movement. AI enthusiasts believe it's possible in theory to make a brain as complex as ours, and when they succeed, it will, almost magically, become conscious. For them the idea of a soul is a non-starter, an artifact of religious history. They think—this is their dogma—that consciousness will emerge quite naturally where there is sufficient computational complexity in the brain's design—as much complexity as in the human brain. Supply the artificial brain with 100 billion artificial neurons (brain cells) and 1000 or more artificial synaptic pathways per neuron; then power it up, and consciousness is bound to emerge. As you can tell, this is 21st century epiphenomenalism.

Remarkably, at least one man is making plans around this concept. Dmitry Itskov, the millionaire "godfather" of Russia's internet, believes he will have the technology to upload his brain to a computer within the next 30 years. This brain, fully conscious because sufficiently complex, will then be uploaded to a robotic body. "For the next few centuries," he explains, "I envision having multiple bodies, one somewhere in space, another hologram-like, my consciousness just moving from one to the other."

Dr. Miguel Nicolelis, a leading neuroscientist working at Duke University, offers a different view of Itskov's "immortality technology":

> You cannot code intuition; you cannot code aesthetic beauty; you cannot code love or hate. There is no way you will ever see a human brain reduced to a digital medium. It's simply impossible to reduce that complexity to the kind of algorithmic process that you will have to have to do that.

And Stuart Hameroff, cofounder of the Center for Consciousness Studies at the University of Arizona and a major pioneer in consciousness theory, denies that computational complexity can explain consciousness. He acknowledges that our most advanced computers are prodigiously intelligent—they can solve complicated problems far faster than we can—but they don't *understand* what they have done, for they are not conscious. Hameroff suspects that consciousness is intrinsic to the universe and has been in it from the beginning, prior to the production of any brain. Even further, it's not unreasonable, he believes, to see consciousness as the *cause* of the universe rather than a latter-day epiphenomenon of the evolutionary process. He does not rule out survival of death in some sort of "quantum soul" and is open to the possibility of reincarnation, largely because of the research of Ian Stevenson (see the chapter on reincarnation).

Ultimately each of us will have to choose between two mysteries. One is the mystery of how human consciousness, including the various kinds of paranormal experience we've explored in earlier chapters, can emerge from brain states in a world without soul. The other is the mystery of how two or more intertwined realities with radically different aptitudes and characteristics, namely body and mind, can interact so harmoniously that they function as one organism living in a single space. I find it easier to live with the second mystery. The first leaves us with a "hard problem" that has escaped solution by the world's best philosophical minds for centuries. We don't see anything in nature that suggests a way out, and the problem seems not only "hard," but insoluble. The second is certainly mysterious, but it makes room for paranormal experience, which the first does not. No wonder materialists are quick to dismiss the near-death experience, reincarnational memories, apparitions, and other-world communication as delusions; their mind-body theories are contradicted by them. Dualism, while not removing their mystery, is roomy enough to account for them. This contrast between what works and what doesn't is radical and far-reaching. It supplies us with one more stick in our bundle.

11.

RELIGION AND THE AFTERLIFE

Our object here is to see what the world's sacred writings, often called scriptures, say about the survival of the human personality beyond death. We want to find out, more particularly, whether there is anything in these scriptures like universal agreement on the subject. Do they sing out victoriously in unison with St. Paul, "O death, where is thy sting? O grave, where is thy victory?" This is the primary question before us here. To a lesser extent we'll concern ourselves with the broad types of afterlife expectations of believers the world over. Finally, and most importantly, we'll consider the relevance of our findings for the modern investigator—parapsychologist, philosopher, theologian, layman—trying to decide whether or not persons do in fact survive. Do the world's scriptures work as evidence?

A scripture is a written document that is accepted by a religion as speaking with authority about matters of ultimate spiritual concern. More often than not a scripture tells the believer about the God or gods he or she is expected to worship. This might include God's active participation in human history.

Some scholars say there are ten scriptures presently in existence. If one insists that before a document can be termed a scripture it must be very ancient (say at least 1000 years old) and have living adherents who hold it sacred, then ten is the correct number. They belong to the traditions we call Hinduism, Buddhism, Jainism, Confucianism, Daoism, Shinto, Judaism, Zoroastrianism, Christianity, and Islam. We'll restrict our attention to the scriptures of these ten traditions. But we should not forget that there are many scriptures of more recent vintage— for example, those written by Sikhs, Baha'is, Mormons, and Spiritists. Though much less ancient, they are as authoritative for the believer of these faiths as, for example, the Veda is for the orthodox Hindu.

Before looking at scriptural samplings below, we should remember that every society, no matter how "primitive," has at least an oral tradition around which it organizes its interpretation of reality. The scriptures we'll be looking at here had their beginnings in oral traditions.

It will be helpful to organize our ten scriptures under three broad categories: religions of the Near East (sometimes called "Western religions"), religions of India, and religions of the Far East.

Religions of the Near East

The scriptures of Zoroastrianism (a religion emerging from Persia, today's Iran, and now nearly extinct except for an area around Mumbai, where there is a Parsi community numbering around 60,000), Christianity, and Islam have fairly well developed eschatologies, or afterlife beliefs. Personal survival is unquestioningly affirmed. Notions of what makes up the surviving personality—whether a resurrected earthly body, a "spiritual body," or a bodiless spirit or soul vary from believer to believer, from sect to sect, and from religion to religion. There is, however, a common affirmation among the scripture of these three traditions: in the final analysis there are two kinds of persons, the saved and the damned. And salvation or damnation is usually thought to be everlasting. The following quotations typify this view:

> And when they [men of evil deeds] approach there where the Judge's Bridge extends, unlike the believing ones of God, who go so firmly forth with me [Zoroaster the prophet] as guide and helper, these shall miss their path and fall, and in the Lie's abode forever shall their habitation be. But for the penitent there is yet hope.... With these shall Ahura [God] dwell.
>
> ZOROASTRIAN AVESTA, GATHAS, YASNA 46.11-12
> (DARMESTETER TRANSLATION)

And when perfection shall have been attained then shall the blow of destruction fall upon the Demon of Falsehood, and the adherents shall perish with her, but swiftest in the happy abode of the Good Mind and of Ahura [God] the righteous saints shall gather, they who proceed in their walk on earth in good repute and honour.

ZOROASTRIAN AVESTA, GATHAS, YASNA 30.10
(DARMESTETER TRANSLATION)

These [evildoers], then, will be sent off to eternal punishment, but the righteous will go to eternal life.

CHRISTIAN NEW TESTAMENT, MATTHEW 25:46
(GOOD NEWS BIBLE)

Just as the weeds are gathered up and burned in the fire, so the same thing will happen at the end of the age: The Son of Man will send out his angels to gather up out of his Kingdom all those who cause people to sin an all others who do evil things, and they will throw them into the fiery furnace, where they will cry and gnash their teeth. Then God's people will shine like the sun in their Father's Kingdom....

CHRISTIAN NEW TESTAMENT, MATTHEW 13:40-43

Woe on that day to the disbelievers who deny the Day of Judgement!... On that day a barrier shall be set between them and their Lord. They shall burn in Hell, and a voice will say to them: "This is the scourge that you denied".... But on that day the faithful will mock the unbelievers as they recline upon their couches and gaze around them. Shall not the unbelievers be rewarded according to their deeds?

MUSLIM KORAN 83 (DAWOOD TRANSLATION)

Many Christians, especially Roman Catholics, believe that souls pass into Purgatory, a region of purification for those not ready to enter the Kingdom of Heaven but also not so wicked as to merit hell. And Muslims often point out that Allah, in his mercy, can forgive the hell dweller if He wishes. In any case, it is clear beyond doubt that the scriptures of Zoroastrianism, Christianity, and Islam emphatically affirm personal survival and hold all of us accountable for our beliefs and deeds.

The case of Judaism is less clear. Most of the writers of the Hebrew Bible (identical to the Protestant version of the Old Testament) assume that some form of existence follows death in a shadowy subterranean realm named Sheol. But life there does not seem to be robust or vital, and there is no separation of the saved from the damned based on their deeds. All apparently undergo the same fate:

> The nether-world [Sheol] from beneath is moved for thee to meet thee at thy coming; the shades are stirred up for thee...All they do answer and say unto thee: 'Art thou also become weak as we? Art thou become like unto us?'

> JEWISH BIBLE, ISAIAH 14:9-10 (JPS 1917 EDITION)

In two places in the Jewish scriptures there is mention of a resurrection of the dead. In the first passage Israelites who are righteous in Jahweh's (God's) eyes will rise out of Sheol:

> Those of our people who have died will live again!
> Their bodies will come back to life.
> All these sleeping in their graves will wake up and sing for joy.
> As the sparkling dew refreshes the earth,
> So the Lord will revive those who have long been dead.

> BIBLE, ISAIAH 26: 19 (GOOD NEWS BIBLE)

In the next passage many of the righteous and the wicked alike will arise, but to different fates:

> And many of them that sleep in the dust of the earth shall awake, some to everlasting life, and some to reproaches and everlasting abhorrence.

> JEWISH BIBLE, DANIEL 12: 2 (JPS 1917 EDITION)

But this idea—which foreshadowed the Christian belief of a general resurrection for all men—was rejected by the author of another book of the Jewish Bible:

The same fate comes to the righteous and the wicked, to the good and the bad, to those who are religious and those who are not.... One fate comes to all alike, and this is as wrong as anything that happens in this world.... The dead know nothing. They have no further reward; they are completely forgotten.

BIBLE, ECCLESIASTES 9: 2-5 (GOOD NEWS BIBLE)

Religions of India

The Hindu, Buddhist, and Jain scriptures are alike in emphasizing that the present life, if lived wisely, is a way-station to a fuller life after death. Survival of death is taken for granted. Although there are important differences in the afterlife doctrines of the three religions, all agree that when we die we are either (1) eternally emancipated or (2) brought to a heavenly or hellish sphere, depending on our karma (deeds), and eventually reborn on earth, hopefully as a human being in a good family. The great majority of persons, according to these scriptures, undergo repeated rebirths on earth until they overcome selfish desires, live wisely, and follow the necessary disciplines taming the ego. Here are some typical passages:

Accordingly, those who are of pleasant conduct here—the prospect is, indeed, that they will enter a pleasant womb, either the womb of a Brahmin, or the womb of a Kshatriya, or the womb of a Vaisya [high castes]. But those who are of stinking conduct here—the prospect is, indeed, that they will enter a stinking womb, either the womb of a dog, or the womb of a swine, or the womb of an outcaste (chandala).

HINDU CHANDOGYA UPANISHAD 5.10.7 (HUME TRANSLATION)

If any man thinks he slays, and if another thinks he is slain, neither knows the ways of truth.... The Eternal in man cannot die.... As a man leaves an old garment and puts on one that is new, the Spirit leaves his mortal body and wanders on to one that is new.

HINDU BHAGAVAD GITA 2:19,22 (MASCARO TRANSLATION)

145

The sinner goes from darkness to darkness, to utter misery; the unholy man who breaks the rule of monks, rushes, as it were, to hell, and to be born again as a brute.

JAIN UTTARADHYAYANA 20.46 (JACOBI TRANSLATION)

Honoured by gods, gandharvas, and men, he [a good Jain pupil] will, on leaving this body which consists of dirt and impurities, become either an eternal Siddha [liberated soul], or a god of great power and small imperfections.

JAIN UTTARADHYAYANA 1.48 (JACOBI TRANSLATION)

Some [at death] enter the womb; evildoers go to hell; the good go to heaven; those free from worldly desires attain nirvana.

BUDDHIST DHAMMAPADA 9.11 (RADHAKRISHNAN TRANSLATION)

When are liberated all
The desires that lodge in one's heart,
Then a mortal becomes immortal!
Then he reaches Brahman!

HINDU KATHA UPANISHAD 6.14 (HUME TRANSLATION)

Freed from all selfish desire, fear, and anger, they live in freedom always. Knowing me [Krishna] as the friend of all creatures, the Lord of the universe, the recipient of worship and spiritual disciplines, they attain eternal peace.

HINDU BHAGAVAD GITA 5,28-29
(EASWARAN AND EDGERTON TRANSLATIONS)

Liberation is the freedom from all karmic matter.... After the soul is released, there remain perfect right belief, perfect right-knowledge, perfect perception, and the state of having accomplished all.

JAIN TATTVARTHADHIGAMA SUTRA 10.2,4
(JAINI-RADHAKRISHNAN TRANSLATION)

A number of monks approached the Lord [Buddha]...these monks spoke this to the Lord: "Revered sir, that young man of family named Punna...has died. What is his bourn, what is his future state?" "Clever, monks, was Punna the young man of family; he followed after dhamma [Buddhist teachings and discipline].... Punna the young man of family has gained final nibbana [nirvana], monks."

BUDDHIST MAJJHIMA NIKAYA 3.270 (HORNER TRANSLATION)

Some scholars have thought that certain passages in the Hindu and Buddhist scriptures left little room for the survival of the person; a few 19th century scholars even went so far as to liken the Buddhist nirvana to annihilation. This, as almost all contemporary Buddhist scholars realize, is completely wrong. The Buddha did teach that there was no self or ego *as we know it* in the final nirvana (parinirvana), but he did not deny the saint's existence. The scriptures leave no doubt on this issue. When a certain Yamaka interprets the Buddha's teaching on nirvana as equivalent to annihilation, he is quickly labeled a "heretic" and receives the following warning:

The Blessed One would never say that on the dissolution of the body the saint who has lost all depravity is annihilated, perishes, and does not exist after death.

BUDDHIST SAMYUTTA NIKAYA 22.85 (WARREN TRANSLATION)

If some of the Buddhist and Hindu scriptures fail to shed much light on the condition of the finally liberated saint, this is because language breaks down: it is unlike anything we know here. Far from implying that the liberated saint ceases to exist, the scriptures instead hint that the state of such a person is inconceivably exalted. Speechlessness does not imply non-existence. It should be noted, however, that Hindus and

Buddhists describe in great detail the afterlives of those who die and do *not* attain liberation. These states of bliss or pain in the various heavens and hells come to an end when karma is exhausted. Then follows another rebirth on earth.

Religions of China and Japan

The oldest and most revered writings of China and Japan are remarkable for their reticence concerning the afterlife. Only the Daoist classic titled the Zhuangzi (Chuang Tzu) tackles the subject in any depth. Yet there are enough hints elsewhere to justify some helpful generalizations.

The writers and compilers of the earliest Chinese classics believed that deceased ancestors were still alive and capable of influencing the living. The ancient Chinese prayed to their various gods, but they also venerated their ancestors and hoped to get blessings from them—and many Chinese still do today. Here is one of the oldest references to what is often referred to as "ancestor worship":

> Abundant is the year, with much millet and much rice,
> And we have tall granaries,
> With hundreds of thousands and millions of units.
> We make wine and sweet spirits
> And offer them to our ancestors, male and female,
> Thus to fulfill all the rites,
> And bring down blessings to all.
>
> BOOK OF ODES, ODE NO. 279
(WING-TSIT CHAN TRANSLATION)

In the later Analects of Confucius, the most revered of all Confucian writings, Confucius refers to spirits, and it is clear he believed in their existence even though he thought it wise to avoid them:

> Tzu Lu asked about the worship of ghosts and spirits. Confucius said: "We don't know yet how to serve men, how can we know about serving the spirits?"
>
> CONFUCIAN ANALECTS 11.11 (DE BARY TRANSLATION)

Fan Ch'ih asked about wisdom. Confucius said: "Devote yourself to the proper demands of the people, respect the ghosts and spirits but keep them at a distance—this may be called wisdom."

CONFUCIAN ANALECTS 6.20 (DE BARY TRANSLATION)

Absent from any of the earliest Confucian writings, including the Analects and the slightly later and much longer Book of Mencius, are references to such ideas as reincarnation, heavens or hells, and otherworldly reward and punishment. When Buddhism reached China in the first century, this metaphysical vacuum was quickly filled, and by the sixth century belief in rebirth and karma was widespread. But these beliefs were imports from India, not native to China's religious imagination.

Daoism is the second great philosophy native to ancient China. Some consider it a religion, but it's really not, though in later centuries it would give birth to one of the world's most complex religions, often referred to as "Religious Daoism." The greatest and earliest of the Daoist classics, the Daodejing (or Tao Te Ching), says nothing and implies nothing about an afterlife belief. But the second greatest, the Zhuangzi (Chuang Tzu), written perhaps two centuries later, speaks often about death and what might lie beyond. Zhuangzi, the author of the book named after him, is renowned for his skepticism on the subject of personal survival, as in these passages:

How do I know that the love of life is not a delusion? And how do I know that the hate of death is not like a man who lost his home when young and does not know where his home is to return to?... People say there is no death. But what is the use? Not only does the physical form disintegrate; the mind also goes with it. Is that not very lamentable?

DAOIST ZHUANGZI, CH. 2 (WING-TSIT CHAN TRANSLATION)

When she [Zhuangzi's wife] first died, do you think I didn't grieve like anyone else? But I looked back to her beginning and the time before she was born.... In the midst of the jumble of wonder and mystery a change took pace and she had a spirit. Another change and she had a body. Another change and she was born. Now there's been another change and she's dead. It's just like the progression of the four seasons, spring, summer, fall, winter.... Now she's going to lie down in a vast room. If I were to follow after her bawling and sobbing, it would show that I don't understand anything about fate. So I stopped.

DAOIST ZHUANGZI, CH. 18 (WATSON TRANSLATION)

The earliest chronicles telling us about Shinto, Japan's indigenous religion, say almost nothing about the state of the dead. The sparse references in the Kojiki and Nihongi (eighth century), do testify, however, to Japanese belief in some form of survival from the earliest historical times. There is, for example, an empty-tomb narrative about one of Japan's great warriors, Yamato-dake no Mikoto. The Nihongi tells how Yamato, soon after his burial, took the shape of a white bird:

At last it soared aloft to Heaven, and there was nothing buried but his clothing and white cap.

SHINTO NIHONGI 7.32 (ASTON TRANSLATION)

But what about the common man? An account of another warrior, Tamichi, much less celebrated and fabulous than Yamato, tells what happened when his grave was dug up:

... a great serpent started up with glaring eyes, and came out of the tomb. It bit the Yemishi, who were [all] afflicted by the serpent's poison, so that many of them died, and one or two escaped. Therefore the men of that time said: "Although dead, Tamichi at last had his revenge. How can it be said that the dead have no knowledge?"

SHINTO NIHONGI 11.30 (ASTON TRANSLATION)

The Nihongi also describes sacrifices to deceased ancestors and human sacrifices at the death of royal personages. Both forcefully suggest some form of belief in personal survival.

Some academics are under the impression that typical Orientals, especially the Chinese, give little thought to an afterlife and are inclined to disbelieve in it. This is perhaps true of the Confucian scholar class, but not of the great majority of Chinese. Over-specializing in the classics we have just looked at, these academics underestimate the impact of Buddhism. This import from otherworldly India had a profound influence on both China and Japan from very early times. Recent studies on Religious Daoism also underscore this mistake. Death in Chinese society meant, at least until Communism under Mao Zedong disrupted the practice of China's religions, becoming an ancestor. The well-respected scholar J. J. M. de Groot wrote around 1900 with very little exaggeration: "What will become of my soul and body after death? is the great question which occupies the minds of the whole Chinese people." Protestant missionary to China Arthur H. Smith, writing about the same time, put it this way:

> The man participating in ancestral worship is constantly projecting himself into the future world; he sees himself in the situations and conditions that he believes his departed ancestors are now in; he also sees himself in relation to the living descendants who later will be called upon to worship him; the guaranteeing of that status in the future life is his central problem.

We began this chapter by asking if the world's ancient sacred writings affirmed the personal survival beyond death. We discovered that the great majority do. Only the earliest Daoist classics leave some doubt. In only one book of the world's scriptures do we see it clearly rejected, the Jewish book Ecclesiastes, and it's only one of 39 books composing the Hebrew Bible. Taken as a whole, the world's earliest sacred writings strongly support personal survival.

What does all this mean? Does it get us any closer to a decision about survival? Is scriptural testimony admissible as evidence? I think the decision turns much more on the evidence we've looked at in earlier chapters, but that it would be a mistake to discount religious belief altogether. Almost all of India's schools of philosophy recognize three means of acquiring valid knowledge (pramānas): direct experience, reason, and scriptural testimony.

What, then, is the reason that the teachings of the world's scriptures remain relevant to us today? The philosopher Jacques Maritain writes:

> ... it is probable that the great and basic ideas, the prime ideas, which are contained in the myths of primitive man, and are handed down in the common heritage of mankind, are more sound than illusory, and deserve respect more than contempt.

The Biblical scholar and theologian Marcus Borg makes the same point:

> A single religious tradition can easily be doubted as merely a human creation and projection, but when one sees that the great religious traditions share much in common, especially at the level of experience and practice, one begins to wonder if there might be something to religion.

Carl Jung supports this insight with some highly original scientific reasoning:

> If we could look into the psyche of the yucca moth, for instance, we would find in it a pattern of ideas...which not only compel the moth to carry out its fertilizing activity on the yucca plant, but help it to "recognize" the total situation. Instinct is anything but a blind and indefinite impulse, since it proves to be attuned and adapted to a definite external situation.

Is belief in survival an instinct, and like other instincts is it "adapted to a definite external situation," namely an actual future life on the other side of death? The near universal testimony of the world's ancient scriptures suggests it is. And the near universal belief in survival encountered by anthropologists in contemporary preliterate societies—societies with rich oral traditions, or "scriptures that never got written"—further suggests it is. But we must not forget that many critics term this idea nothing more than a widespread—a near universal—fiction, the product of a neurosis growing out of the fear of extinction at death, and one that modern, "evolved" men and women are supposedly in the process of outgrowing. They tell us, in the words of Clarence Darrow, an earlier critic, that "nature creates many desires which she does not satisfy; most of the wishes of men meet no fruition."

Nevertheless, the universality of the idea of survival is an impressive fact. An idea's universality is not enough to establish its validity, but it is a far from negligible consideration for seekers after truth who want as much information on the subject of survival as they can get. Is it impressive enough to add to our collection of sticks? Even though it doesn't have nearly the strength of the other ones, I'm tempted to. I'll leave the decision to the reader.

CONCLUSION

One of the most revolutionary ideas ever conceived is that we are more than our bodies and that our true home lies beyond our physical planet. This idea—that we are or have souls that do not die at death—is found in all the earth's religions. Under attack since The Enlightenment, it is reemerging in our own day as a revolutionary idea for a materialist culture. It is evidence in support of this idea that we have been looking at here.

This idea has had a profound impact on civilization throughout human history up to our own day. It has inspired many, if not most, of the great works of art: the Pyramids, the Parthenon, Chartres Cathedral, Bach's Mass in B Minor, the Bhagavad Gita, the Bible; the list goes on and on. But too often it reaches us today in a form that is primitive and even dangerous. That we continue to be influenced by these worn-out theologies of eternal damnation for some and divinely favored fates for others is unworthy of us, especially since we now have teachers and guides telling us what really happens. If only we would listen to them, this is what our world would look like:

- It would lead to a rejection of primitive theologies that have lacked guidance from spirit teachers closer to the Divine Source and to a restoration of confidence in the reality and wise governance of the universe by that Source.
- It would instill in many a belief that life is "going somewhere" or "adding up to something." It would build confidence in a Source

of immense proportions at the helm of a soul-building process that would give our lives meaning they wouldn't otherwise have.

• It would lead to a confident expectation that life wouldn't end at death, that those cut off early in life would not be denied their share, and that ancestors and their descendants would be reunited.

• It would remove the dullness of afterlife conceptions that comes from thinking of it as static, even boring, with nothing more left to achieve; or vague, with nothing concrete and colorful and beautiful to recommend it. The heavens would be reconceived as a challenging, stimulating, dynamic environment.

• It would help remove the anguish of those mourning the death of a child, for they would know their loved one was in good hands.

• It would lift the melancholy that fear of personal extinction brings to many people, especially the elderly.

• It would make rational the near universal instinct to pray and help alleviate loneliness and despair in the face of personal tragedy.

• It would lead to the conviction that good actions meet with a happy destiny and selfish or criminal actions with the opposite. This "law of karma" has through the centuries provided the glue that helps societies stay more or less law-abiding.

• It would give young people the incentive to get serious about their lives and give back something meaningful to the world before it's too late. The law of karma would help awaken responsible action.

• Active seniors would be more likely to volunteer their time in classrooms and give lagging students one-on-one attention. And our youth would in turn be more likely to visit the disabled and ailing elderly in their nursing homes. The growing perception of a link between loving service to one's neighbor and the outcome after death would gradually change all of society for the better.

• Suicide would be discouraged in the world's collective consciousness by thoughts of its karmic consequences and would be less likely to occur anyway in a better, happier world.

• To the extent that the law of karma is taken seriously, it would lead to less crime, fewer prisoners, and more tax dollars for education, infrastructure repair, and green technology.

• To the extent that it is taken seriously, it would discourage those near death from taking heroic measures to extend their lives a few more weeks—a costly choice that grows out of the fear that this is the only life there is, and that, according to most authorities, the world cannot afford.

- To the extent that it is taken seriously and replaces the one-life-is-all-you-get philosophy so prevalent among the super-rich, it would discourage rampant greed and encourage a spirituality of compassion. More billionaires would join Warren Buffet's Billionaire Club, and the enormous contrast between the wealthy and the impoverished of the world would be attenuated.
- Consumption of the world's resources would be reduced as people came to see that this isn't their only chance at happiness.
- Racism and sexism would become less enticing once society came to better understand that souls have no color or sex.
- The worldview unveiled here would uplift women as the Divine Source was elevated beyond maleness, and sex change between lives was recognized as normal.
- A greater emphasis on the soul would discourage the present fixation on the body and create more psychological space for deeper reflection and more wholesome pursuits.
- It would attract materialist-oriented scientists to a worldview devoid of supernatural absurdities and replace them with a worldview governed by natural law—a natural law encompassing not only our physical world but our environment on the other side of death as well. A new science of astral matter, already begun, would ripen.
- It would lead to a renewed emphasis on music education and the arts in general as funds became available for a better life.
- Our world would become more interesting once we recognize that it is visited by spirits we cannot see; it would "verticalize" our world.
- Fundamentalist religion would lose much of its appeal as the more spacious, inclusive religion based on insights given us by our spirit friends gained traction. Just as there is one science and not many, in the same way there would be one religion, although with many faces growing out of the world's various cultures. There would still be wars, but they wouldn't as easily get mixed up with religion.
- Certain forms of mental illness would be properly diagnosed as having a spiritual etiology and would be appropriately treated. This treatment would bring relief to thousands of patients locked up in mental hospitals and to their families.

On the other hand, the soul theory can become perverted if carried too far. It can lead to an otherworldliness that discourages a healthy commitment to bettering and enjoying our present world. Even worse, it can lead to a contempt for life—as seen in the present wave of suicide bombers, all of whom expect to enter a better place when death is hastened.

Also, some people, not many actually, claim they would prefer only this one life rather than have to deal with another one following. So for them a soul would be an impediment to happiness.

Still others ("atheistic existentialists") claim that the expectation of another life would belittle the importance of this one, thereby removing the urgency of living this one to the fullest.

Human beings, at their best, are more than unthinking consumers. They wonder about the meaning of life; they are philosophers; they are moral agents. The conclusions they reach have far-reaching consequences, as the above bullet points make clear. These conclusions are endlessly debatable. Looking at both sides of a Big Question like the one proposed here—do we survive death? —introduces them to their own creative depths, teaches them how to reason and defend a point, and gives them a taste, perhaps their first, of the joy of living in the mind. In a word, it humanizes them.

But of greatest importance to some of us—both those who would love to live beyond death and those who wouldn't—is the question of truth. What does the evidence actually show? Some of us would prefer to know the answer, however it turns out, and deal with it, whatever it entails. This book has provided evidence for the soul, without which an afterlife would be impossible. This evidence has come mainly from consciousness research, with emphasis on the paranormal. By now readers should be in a good position to make up their own minds.

I have made up mine, and it would be overly cautious of me to hold back my personal conclusion. So here goes.

First let me acknowledge an appreciation of my secularist friends for discarding the old Sunday school formula of a jealous God who sends us all to heaven or hell for eternity. They rightly point out, often with passion, why this foolishness doesn't work. Having said this, it is with disappointment that I view their unwillingness to question their too hasty assumptions about the soul and a different kind of afterlife. Sam Goldwyn famously said, "Don't confuse me with facts. I've already made up my mind." This quotation applies not only to religious fundamentalists whom secularists belittle, but all too often to secularists themselves.

The facts I think they should be examining are the ones we've uncovered here. If their minds were as open as they would like to believe, they would have to question their convictions about an afterlife as they survey the imposing evidence coming at them from all sides. They would find nothing here to dissuade them from dismissing simplistic religious formulas, but the new science of afterlife study presented here would check their tendency to throw out everything that doesn't tally with their equally simplistic materialist formulas. Difficult it will be for secularists or materialists or physicalists—whatever name they might prefer—to differentiate this science from the religious dogmas they rightly outgrew. I am well aware that the evidence provided here might arouse for some of them a feeling of falling into a deep sinkhole, a sinkhole they had climbed out of in their youth.

What I believe they fear is a return to religion, but the evidence we've looked at here doesn't grow out of religion. An afterlife is not necessarily any more religious than this life. The same goes for the self that survives death. A surviving self and an afterlife that the self survives into are just the way things are. We learn of them not from scripture, but from science.

The way things are. How sure can we be of this? Let's look back for a minute, back to the chapter on poltergeists. Can a physicalist account for the stone-throwing game? No. All he can say in defense of himself is that the case is a fraud. But that requires him to believe that David Fontana, a renowned parapsychologist and scholarly author over the course of a long life, is a charlatan and a liar—a ridiculous claim. Or look back to the chess game played between the living and the deceased grand masters. Or consider the thousands of book tests performed to test the accuracy of what came forth from mediums supposedly channeling spirits. The materialist has no answer for any of this. The same goes for the cases covered in the chapters on deathbed visions, the near-death experience, apparitions, spirit attachment, reincarnation cases, and instrumental transcommunication. Materialists try not to think of all this, but if they do, they tell themselves that someday real science, not pseudoscience, will figure it all out. Until that happens, they'll stick to their guns. Until death solves the riddle even for them.

As I see it, if the case of the poltergeist "Pete" and his stone-throwing game were the only case of its type on record, I'd be looking beyond materialism for answers *on that basis alone.* But there are *dozens* of impressive poltergeist cases on record. Further, we have only to look at the evidence from surveillance cameras to see that materialism has no way of explaining such phenomena.

But the dualist account of human nature does a lot better. Something that we cannot see and that is intelligent is at work. And those intelligences are in most cases former human beings. How sure can we be of this? If you assign a 90% probability of the survival claim being correct based on evidence presented in each of the first eight chapters ("Deathbed Visions" through "ITC"), you get a probability against error of 10^8, or one in a hundred million. If you find only three types of evidence convincing, you still get a probability against error of 10^3, or one in a thousand.

As I see it, the case for survival has been proved beyond a reasonable doubt. Its truth does not hinge on wishful thinking, as materialists like to claim. It hinges on evidence. It doesn't depend on any particular religion's teaching, as some religious people like to claim. It depends on evidence. It doesn't require that one ignore the evidence of science. It requires that one look at *all* of science, including the new science of consciousness.

The English poet Philip Larkin wrote the late 20th century's greatest lament over death, "Aubade." In it he voices the cry of a generation of well-educated Brits caught between a religion that wasn't working (Anglicanism) and a false science that canonized materialism. Larkin was not acquainted with the evidence presented here, and his poem shows it. Lying sleepless in his bed just before dawn, he tell us how "the dread /Of dying, and being dead,/ Flashes afresh to hold and horrify." It's not remorse over mistakes made in life that makes him shudder, but

... the total emptiness forever,
The sure extinction that we travel to
And shall be lost in always. Not to be here,
Not to be anywhere,
And soon; nothing more terrible, nothing more true.

And what does this nothingness amount to?

... no sight, no sound,
No touch or taste or smell, nothing to think with,
Nothing to love or link with,
The anesthetic from which none come round.

Another European, the early 20ᵗʰ century Belgian essayist and playwright Maurice Maeterlinck, tells a very different story. Unlike Larkin, he had studied the early writings of psychical researchers and rejected materialism. Here he tells a story I have never forgotten, the story of a mother who had lost her only son, the pride and joy of her life:

The other day I went to see a woman whom I knew before the war—she was happy then—and who had lost her only son in one of the battles in the Argonne [during World War I]. She was a widow, almost a poor woman; and, now that this son, her pride and joy, was no more, she no longer had any reason for living. I hesitated to knock on her door. Was I not about to witness one of those hopeless griefs at whose feet all words fall to the ground like shameful and insulting lies? Which of us today is not familiar with these mournful interviews, this dismal duty?

To my great astonishment, she handed me her hand with a kindly smile. Her eyes, to which I hardly dared raise my own, were free of tears.

"You have come to speak of him," she said, in a cheerful tone, and it was as if her voice had grown younger.

"Alas, yes! I had heard of your sorrow, and I have come...."

"Yes, I too believed that my unhappiness was irreparable; but now I know that he is not dead."

"What! He is not dead? Do you mean that the news...? But I thought that the body..."

"Yes, his body is over there; and I have even a photograph of the grave. Let me show it to you. See, that fourth cross on the left, that fourth cross; that is where he is lying. One of his friends, who buried him, sent me this card and gave me all the details. He suffered no pain. There was not even a death struggle. And he has told me so himself. He is quite astonished that death should be so easy, so slight a thing...You do not understand? Yes, I see what it is; you are just as I used to be, as all the others are. I do not explain the matter to the others; what would be the use? They do not wish to understand. But you, you will understand. He is more alive than he ever was; he is free and happy. He does just as he likes. He tells me that one cannot imagine what a release death is, what a weight it removes from you, nor the joy which it brings. He comes to see me when I call him. He loves, especially, to come in the evening; and we chat as we used to. He has not altered; he is just as he was on the day he went away, only younger, stronger, handsomer. We have never been happier, more united, nearer to one another. He divines my thoughts before I utter them. He knows everything; he sees everything; but he cannot tell me everything he knows. He maintains that I must be wanting to follow him and that I must wait for my hour. And, while I wait, we are living in a happiness greater than that which was ours before the war, a happiness which nothing can ever trouble again."

Those about her pitied the poor woman; and, as she did not weep, as she was gay and smiling, they believed her mad.

All that we have surveyed in this book leaves me with the conviction that she was far from mad, but, quite the reverse, she was blessed with a sanity that we can only admire and marvel at. It is my hope that the evidence presented here, from so many sticks bundled together, has left you with a similar conviction and that you will go out and spread the word.

INDEX

Paperbacks also available from
White Crow Books

Elsa Barker—*Letters from a Living Dead Man*
ISBN 978-1-907355-83-7

Elsa Barker—*War Letters from the Living Dead Man*
ISBN 978-1-907355-85-1

Elsa Barker—*Last Letters from the Living Dead Man*
ISBN 978-1-907355-87-5

Richard Maurice Bucke—
Cosmic Consciousness
ISBN 978-1-907355-10-3

Stafford Betty—
The Imprisoned Splendor
ISBN 978-1-907661-98-3

Stafford Betty—
Heaven and Hell Unveiled: Updates from the World of Spirit.
ISBN 978-1-910121-30-6

Ineke Koedam—
In the Light of Death: Experiences on the threshold between life and death
ISBN 978-1-910121-48-1

Arthur Conan Doyle with Simon Parke—
Conversations with Arthur Conan Doyle
ISBN 978-1-907355-80-6

Meister Eckhart with Simon Parke—
Conversations with Meister Eckhart
ISBN 978-1-907355-18-9

D. D. Home—*Incidents in my Life Part 1*
ISBN 978-1-907355-15-8

Mme. Dunglas Home; edited, with an Introduction, by Sir Arthur Conan Doyle—*D. D. Home: His Life and Mission*
ISBN 978-1-907355-16-5

Edward C. Randall—
Frontiers of the Afterlife
ISBN 978-1-907355-30-1

Rebecca Ruter Springer—
Intra Muros: My Dream of Heaven
ISBN 978-1-907355-11-0

Leo Tolstoy, edited by Simon Parke—*Forbidden Words*
ISBN 978-1-907355-00-4

Erlendur Haraldsson and Loftur Gissurarson—
Indridi Indridason: The Icelandic Physical Medium
ISBN 978-1-910121-50-4

Goerge E. Moss—
Earth's Cosmic Ascendancy: Spirit and Extraterrestrials Guide us through Times of Change
ISBN 978-1-910121-28-3

Steven T. Parsons and Callum E. Cooper—
Paracoustics: Sound & the Paranormal
ISBN 978-1-910121-32-0

L. C. Danby—
The Certainty of Eternity: The Story of Australia's Greatest Medium
ISBN 978-1-910121-34-4

Madelaine Lawrence —
The Death View Revolution: A Guide to Transpersonal Experiences Surrounding Death
ISBN 978-1-910121-37-5

Zofia Weaver—
Other Realities?: The enigma of Franek Kluski's mediumship
ISBN 978-1-910121-39-9

Roy L. Hill—
Psychology and the Near-Death Experience: Searching for God
ISBN 978-1-910121-42-9

Tricia. J. Robertson —
"Things You Can do When You're Dead!: True Accounts of After Death Communication"
ISBN 978-1-908733-60-3

Tricia. J. Robertson —
More Things you Can do When You're Dead: What Can You Truly Believe?
ISBN 978-1-910121-44-3

Jody Long—
God's Fingerprints: Impressions of Near-Death Experiences
ISBN 978-1-910121-05-4

Leo Tolstoy with Simon Parke—
Conversations with Tolstoy
ISBN 978-1-907355-25-7

Howard Williams with an Introduction by Leo Tolstoy—*The Ethics of Diet: An Anthology of Vegetarian Thought*
ISBN 978-1-907355-21-9

Vincent Van Gogh with Simon Parke—*Conversations with Van Gogh*
ISBN 978-1-907355-95-0

Wolfgang Amadeus Mozart with Simon Parke—*Conversations with Mozart*
ISBN 978-1-907661-38-9

Jesus of Nazareth with Simon Parke—*Conversations with Jesus of Nazareth*
ISBN 978-1-907661-41-9

Thomas à Kempis with Simon Parke—*The Imitation of Christ*
ISBN 978-1-907661-58-7

Julian of Norwich with Simon Parke—*Revelations of Divine Love*
ISBN 978-1-907661-88-4

Allan Kardec—*The Spirits Book*
ISBN 978-1-907355-98-1

Allan Kardec—*The Book on Mediums*
ISBN 978-1-907661-75-4

Emanuel Swedenborg—*Heaven and Hell*
ISBN 978-1-907661-55-6

P.D. Ouspensky—*Tertium Organum: The Third Canon of Thought*
ISBN 978-1-907661-47-1

Dwight Goddard—*A Buddhist Bible*
ISBN 978-1-907661-44-0

Michael Tymn—*The Afterlife Revealed*
ISBN 978-1-970661-90-7

Michael Tymn—*Transcending the Titanic: Beyond Death's Door*
ISBN 978-1-908733-02-3

Guy L. Playfair—*If This Be Magic*
ISBN 978-1-907661-84-6

Guy L. Playfair—*The Flying Cow*
ISBN 978-1-907661-94-5

Guy L. Playfair —*This House is Haunted: The True Story of the Enfield Poltergeist*
ISBN 978-1-907661-78-5

Carl Wickland, M.D.—*Thirty Years Among the Dead*
ISBN 978-1-907661-72-3

John E. Mack—*Passport to the Cosmos*
ISBN 978-1-907661-81-5

Peter & Elizabeth Fenwick—*The Truth in the Light*
ISBN 978-1-908733-08-5

Erlendur Haraldsson— *Modern Miracles*
ISBN 978-1-908733-25-2

Erlendur Haraldsson— *At the Hour of Death*
ISBN 978-1-908733-27-6

Erlendur Haraldsson—*The Departed Among the Living*
ISBN 978-1-908733-29-0

Brian Inglis—*Science and Parascience*
ISBN 978-1-908733-18-4

Brian Inglis—*Natural and Supernatural: A History of the Paranormal*
ISBN 978-1-908733-20-7

Ernest Holmes—*The Science of Mind*
ISBN 978-1-908733-10-8

Victor & Wendy Zammit —*A Lawyer Presents the Evidence For the Afterlife*
ISBN 978-1-908733-22-1

Casper S. Yost—*Patience Worth: A Psychic Mystery*
ISBN 978-1-908733-06-1

William Usborne Moore—*Glimpses of the Next State*
ISBN 978-1-907661-01-3

William Usborne Moore—*The Voices*
ISBN 978-1-908733-04-7

John W. White—*The Highest State of Consciousness*
ISBN 978-1-908733-31-3

Lord Dowding—*Many Mansions*
ISBN 978-1-910121-07-8

Paul Pearsall, Ph.D. —*Super Joy*
ISBN 978-1-908733-16-0

All titles available as eBooks, and selected titles available in Hardback and Audiobook formats from www.whitecrowbooks.com